Random Access: Photographs by John T. Hill

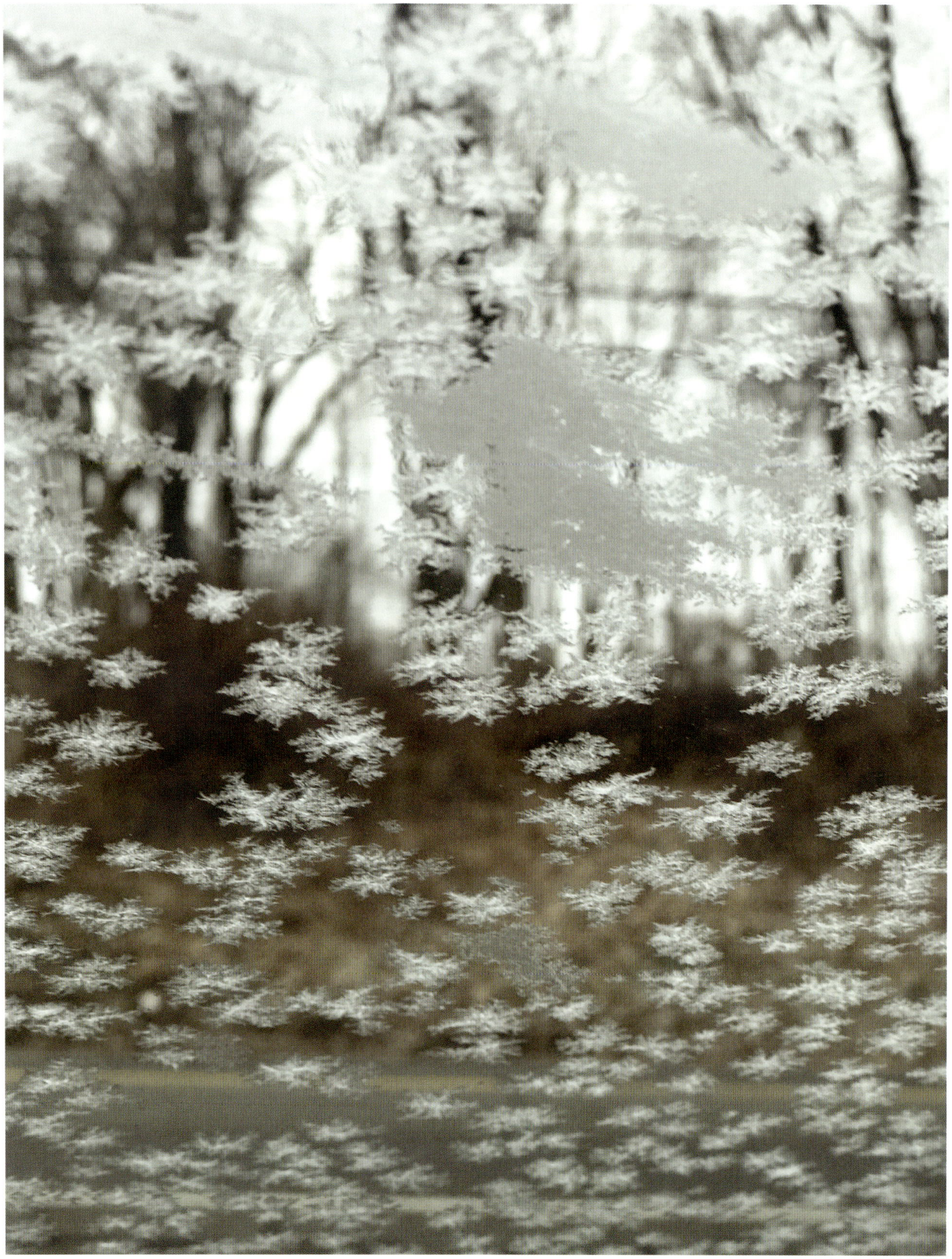

Random Access: Photographs by John T. Hill

Spanning 70 years

Foreword Stephen V. Kobasa

Preface John T. Hill

Introduction Corinne A. Forti

Essay Kathy Leonard Czepiel

Steidl

Foreword

What does it mean to be the most democratic of photographers? In John Hill's images we do not find the self-congratulation of "Look at what only I can see," but rather, the open invitation of "This is what you also are capable of seeing." He offers lessons in both curiosity and generosity, a humane vision of things that does not sentimentalize, but celebrates the contradictions and uncertainties of the world we find ourselves in. In the links he fashions between locale and character that are the subject of so much of his work, it is made brilliantly apparent that we learn who we are through the places where we choose to be.

Stephen Vincent Kobasa, May 13, 2022

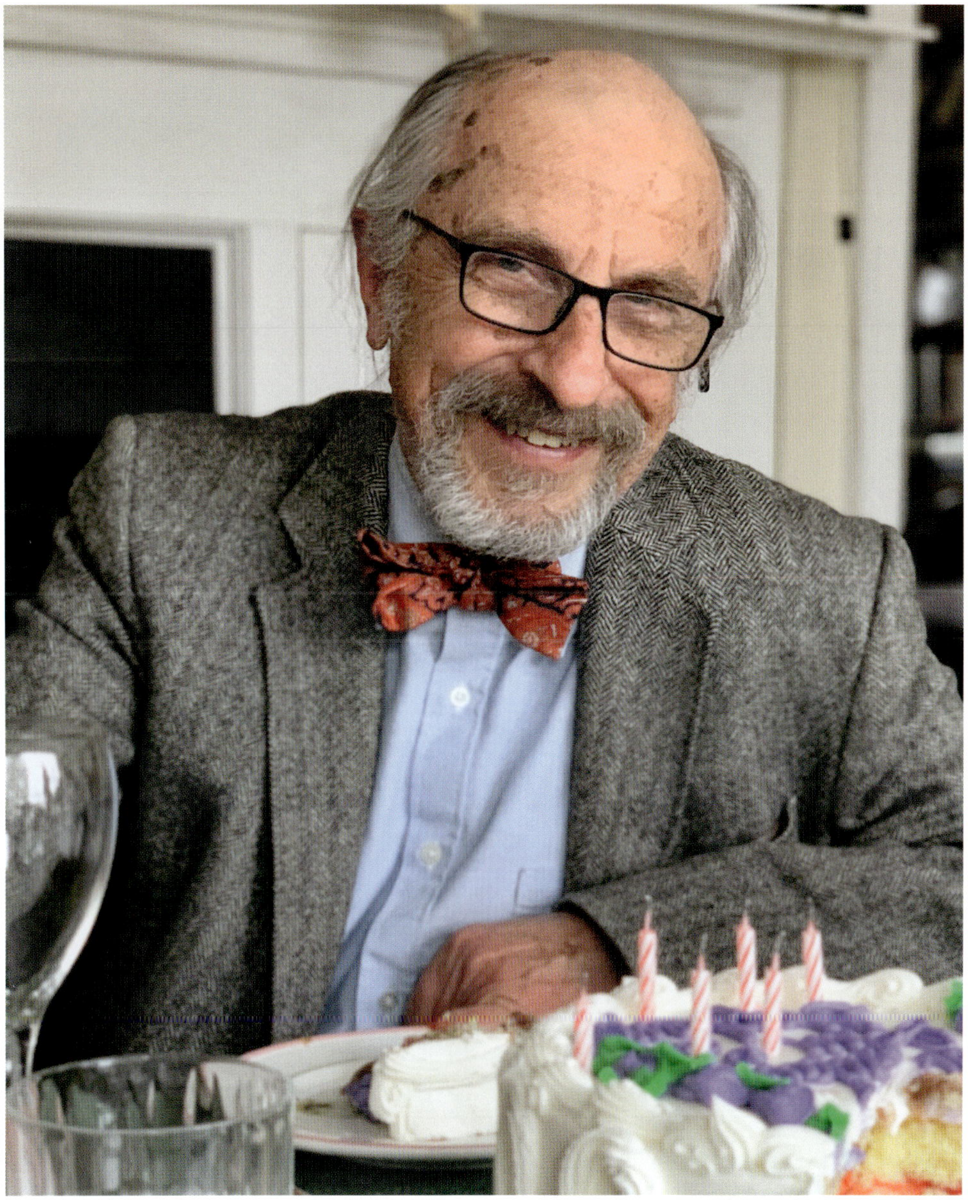

Stephen Vincent Kobasa, 2022

Preface

Two artists worthy of great respect are Louis Armstrong and Pablo Picasso. They both said what most artists believe:

> *"If you have to ask what jazz is,*
> *you'll never know."*
> Louis Armstrong

> *"You don't make art, you find it."*
> Pablo Picasso

If you need to explain the work, it is likely that no words will ever fill the void created by the absence of an innate visual gift. Like music's ineffability, it cannot be put into words. The work must speak for itself.

When I'm holding a camera, I am receptive to whatever I may find most provocative. Baudelaire described this in his account of the *flaneur*, that person who goes out with an open eye and mind.

My goal is to record chance happenings that strike a personal visual chord. In these photographs, what drives me are two things. One is selecting a worthy subject. The second is to create a visual tension.

Position, size and brightness are the primal elements driving all visual works.

John T. Hill

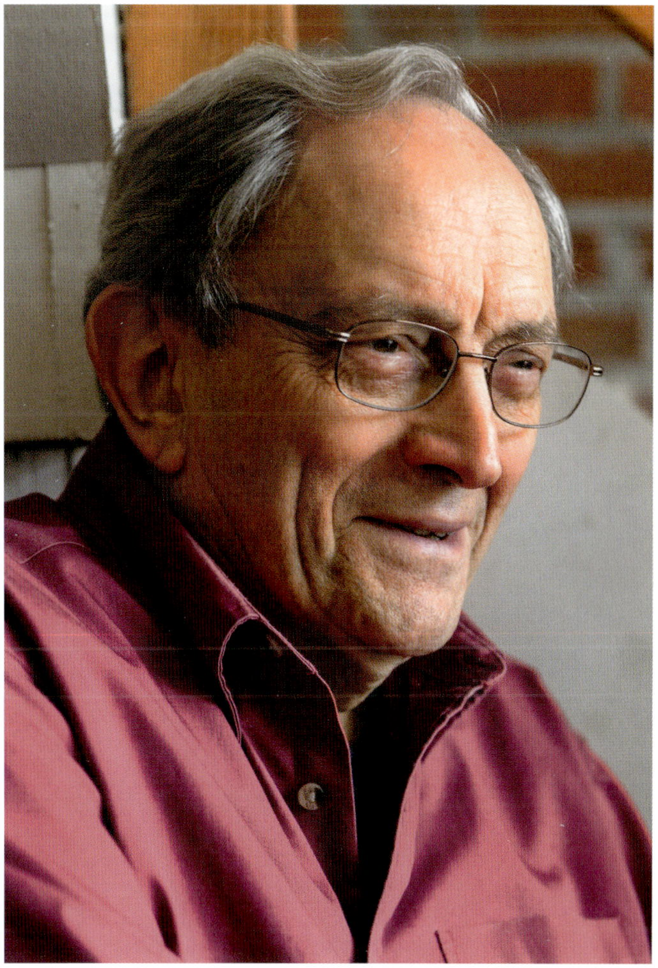

Photo by Jennifer Jane Prushinski, 2018

Introduction

Random Access by John T. Hill

Time fragments to intrigue and provoke.

Simple images that stimulate the imagination
to invite new meanings.

These photographs, taken over 70 years, are
indeed random. The collection is defined
by visceral images, each inspiring personal readings.
No explanation is offered.

Following are two examples:

During a peaceful May Day protest in 1970, a
young African American boy looks directly at the
camera wearing a badge "Human Rights,
Not Violence" defying the political sentiments of
the 1970s.

The second is a glimpse of a major New York
artery seen over a flower balanced on a stack
of books, raising questions and evoking deep
feelings.

The iconic American photographer Walker Evans
said it best:

"The eye traffics in feelings, not in thoughts."

Corinne A Forti, John T. Hill observer for 52 years

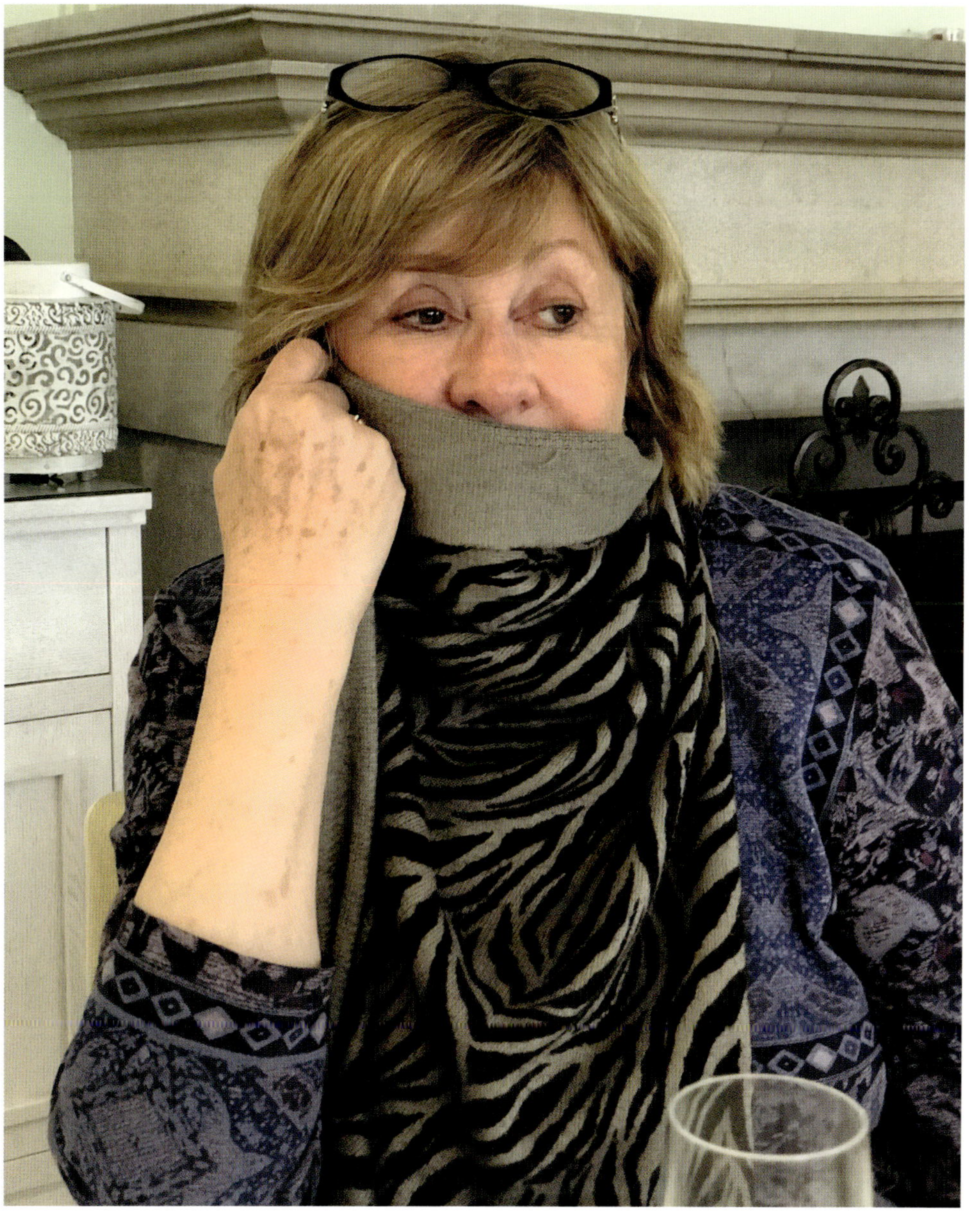

Corinne A. Forti, Porto, Portugal, 2018

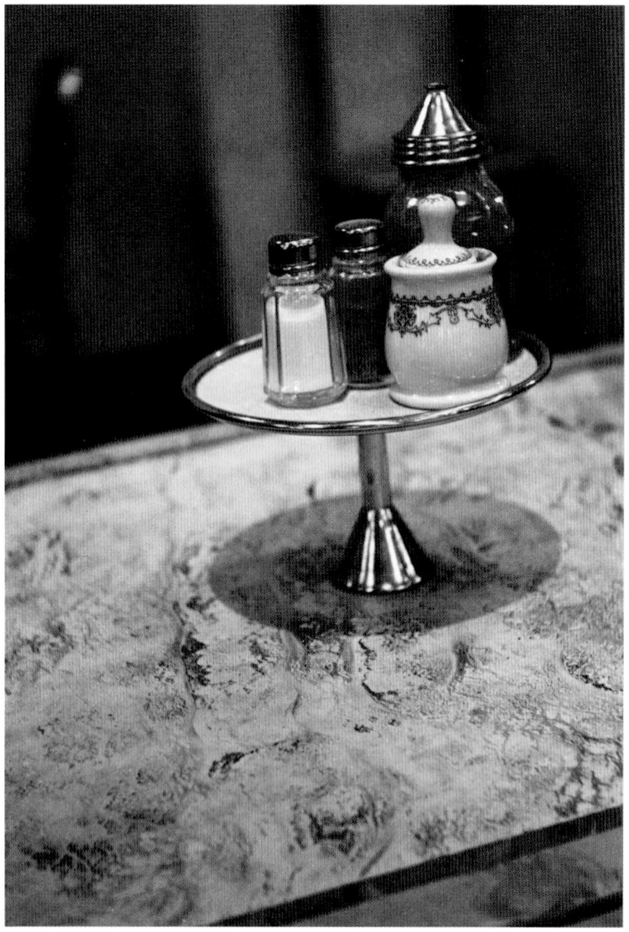

Condiments, Horn & Hardart Automat, 1958

Pause Effect

by Kathy Leonard Czepiel

Even before the rise of the internet and social media, "The speed with which the world went by us was not, I think, particularly considerate of pausing," Stephen Kobasa says. But pausing is exactly what he hopes viewers will do when they encounter the photography of New Haven's John T. Hill recently exhibited at the Institute Library in New Haven, CT.

As a "persistent observer," Hill catalogs what he calls "found compositions," as if the world were doing the composing for him. "His eye is just so keen, and he convinces you that you could see these things, too," says Kobasa, a longtime friend of Hill's who is also an arts writer and political activist. "There are some photographers that make pictures that say to you, 'You wouldn't have seen this. Only I would have seen this.' But John's not like that... His work is always an invitation in some way to join him in this exercise of attention."

Sometimes Hill makes what might be labeled street photography, capturing ordinary people in action, like a little boy who's about to leap over a puddle and out of the frame of Piazza Navona, Rome, December, 1964. None of the other people on the cobbled piazza are watching him, though the puddles themselves stand in as eyes, reflecting the hand of a statue on the side of a nearby fountain, a man on a ladder arranging a shop display, a portion of the boy's leg. While everyone else is turned away, the statue and the boy are in the foreground, turned toward the viewer as if to draw us into the fleeting scene.

Even in Hill's portraits, his subjects are treated more like elements in a larger composition. A young man in Savin Rock, Connecticut, 1964 wears a classic look of the time: white T-shirt, pompadour hairstyle, cynical gaze directed at the camera. His full lips are closed, but in the background, the open-mouthed façade of the park's Laff in the Dark ride opens its big-toothed grin as if to chomp down on him. Another portrait, Farm wife, Jackson County, Georgia, ca. 1952, features Hill's own grand-mother. "She was quite a presence," Hill recalls. "A tough lady." In a deceptively simple kitchen tableau, her aged hand reaches into a four-point composition formed by her pale face, a large jar of buttermilk and a white bowl and mug.

More often, Hill's photographs—at least the ones Kobasa has chosen—are devoid of people, perhaps the result of his 30 years working as a corporate photographer for clients including J.P. Morgan and IBM, while teaching at Yale. In one of the exhibition's few color photographs, Billboard, Queens, New York (undated), the shape of a bank of bright yellow signs lettered in red and black is echoed by a brick building striped with windows reflecting a cloudy sky. What the signs say is less interesting than how they say it, in chunky, matching sans-serif font lit with an orange glow. The interplay of architectural forms is striking, too, in Atlantic City, New Jersey, 1975. Here, the bare metal frames of beach canopies in the off-season play against the marching lines of a boardwalk making its own angular curve along the sand. Stabilizing the image are its two horizons: edge of sand and edge of ocean.

One of Hill's greatest legacies is his role as co-founder of the photography department at the Yale School of Art. He began teaching photography there in 1960, upon his graduation, when it was still a subset of the graphic design program. By the early 1970s, critics, merchants and dealers had discovered photography's commercial potential, Hill says, and students wanted to study photography exclusively. So, with his colleague Alvin Eisenman, Hill created and launched a separate, successful department.

Another of Hill's Yale colleagues was the photographer Walker Evans, who asked Hill to be the executor of his estate, which included a valuable collection of 20,000 of the artist's negatives. Hill served in that role for 19 years before arranging the collection's acquisition by the Metropolitan Museum of Art in 1994. He has written and compiled numerous books on Evans's work, some of which are also on display in the Institute Library exhibition, along with books he wrote, edited or designed on the artists Edward Weston, Erwin Hauer, Norman Ives, Peter Sekaer and William E. Crawford.

Hill's own work is held by the Bibliothéque Nationale in Paris and has been exhibited at the Yale University Art Gallery. "He's been such an advocate for so many other artists, especially photographers," Kobasa says, adding that "it was time" to turn more attention back on the artist himself, who continues to make photographs today. "I'm pursuing whatever I see that fascinates me," Hill says—whatever the world has composed for him.

Published by The Daily Nutmeg
November 23, 2021

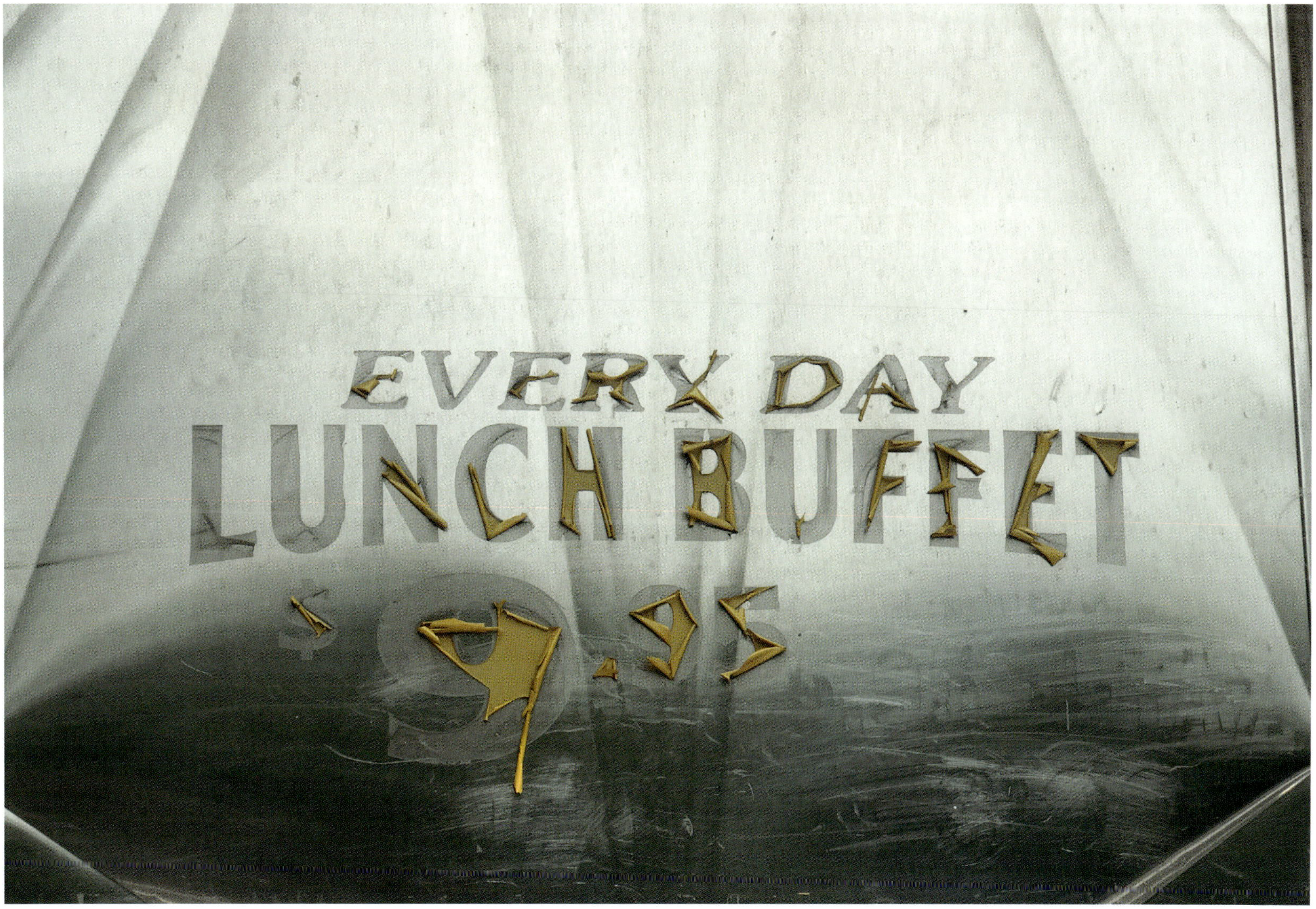

Tandoor Indian Restaurant, Chapel Street, New Haven, Connecticut, 2019

14

Farm Wife, Jackson County, Georgia, 1952

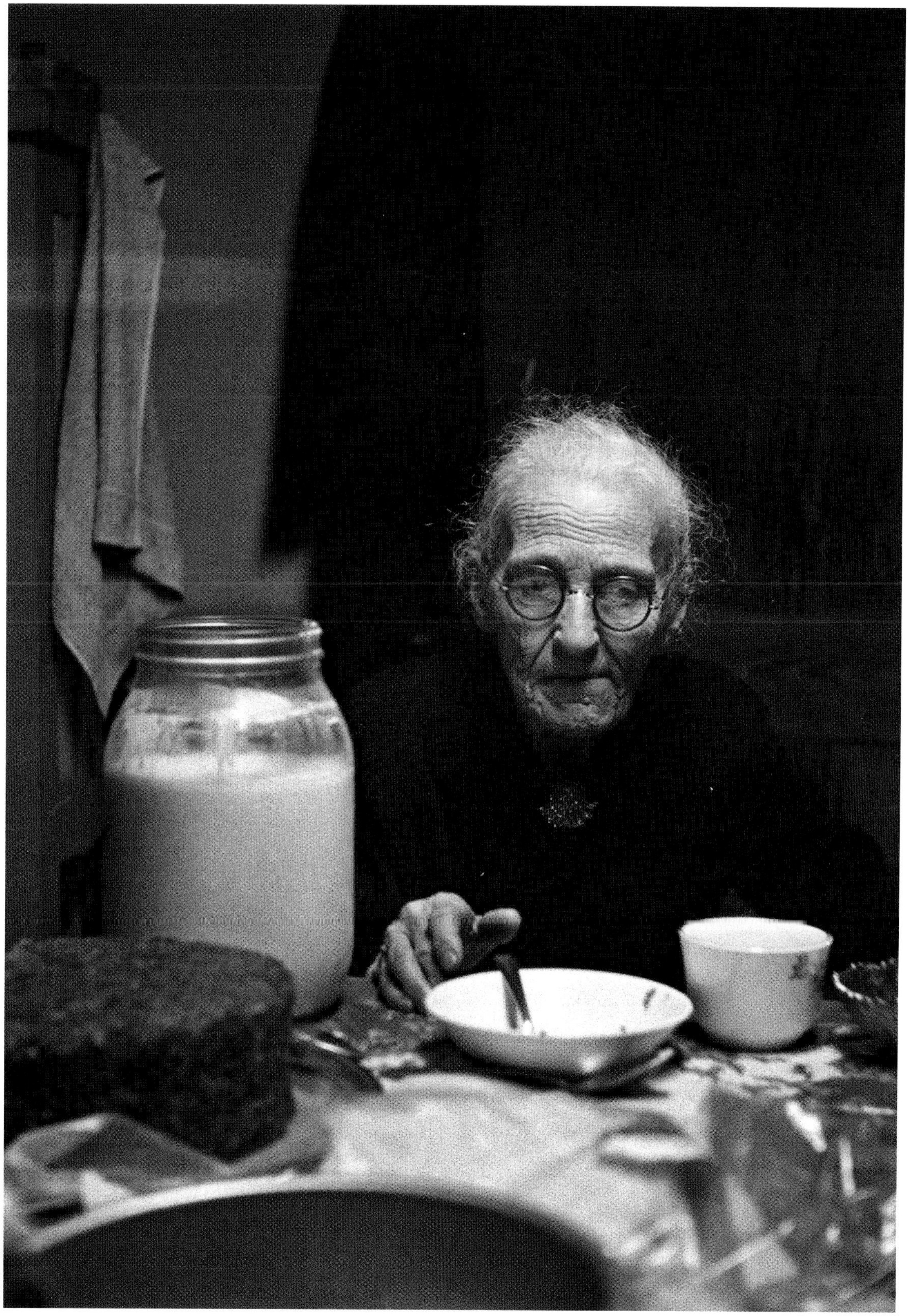

16

Small Circus, Fairground Street, Marietta, Georgia, 1952

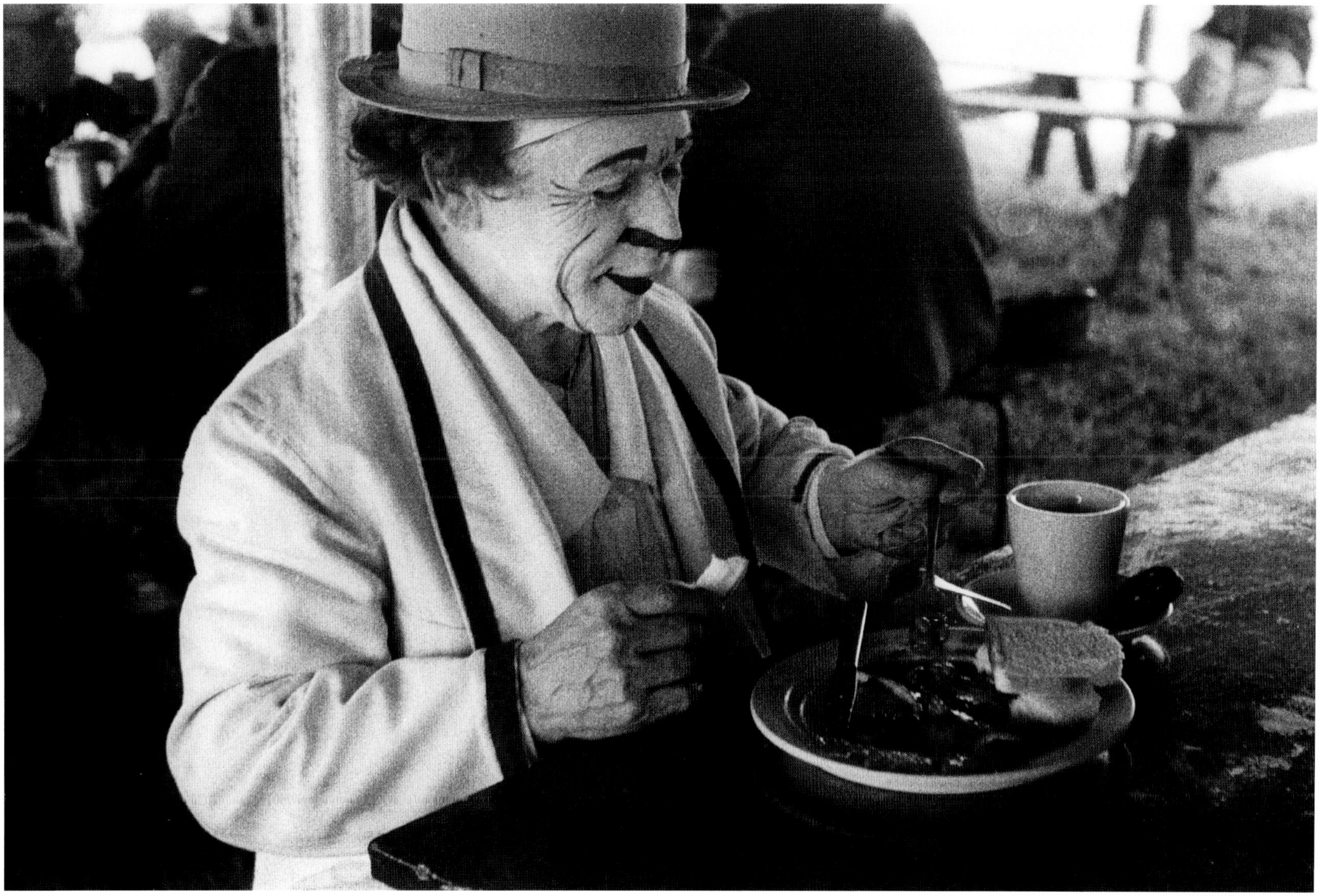

18

Savin Rock Beach, Connecticut, After Storm, September, 1958

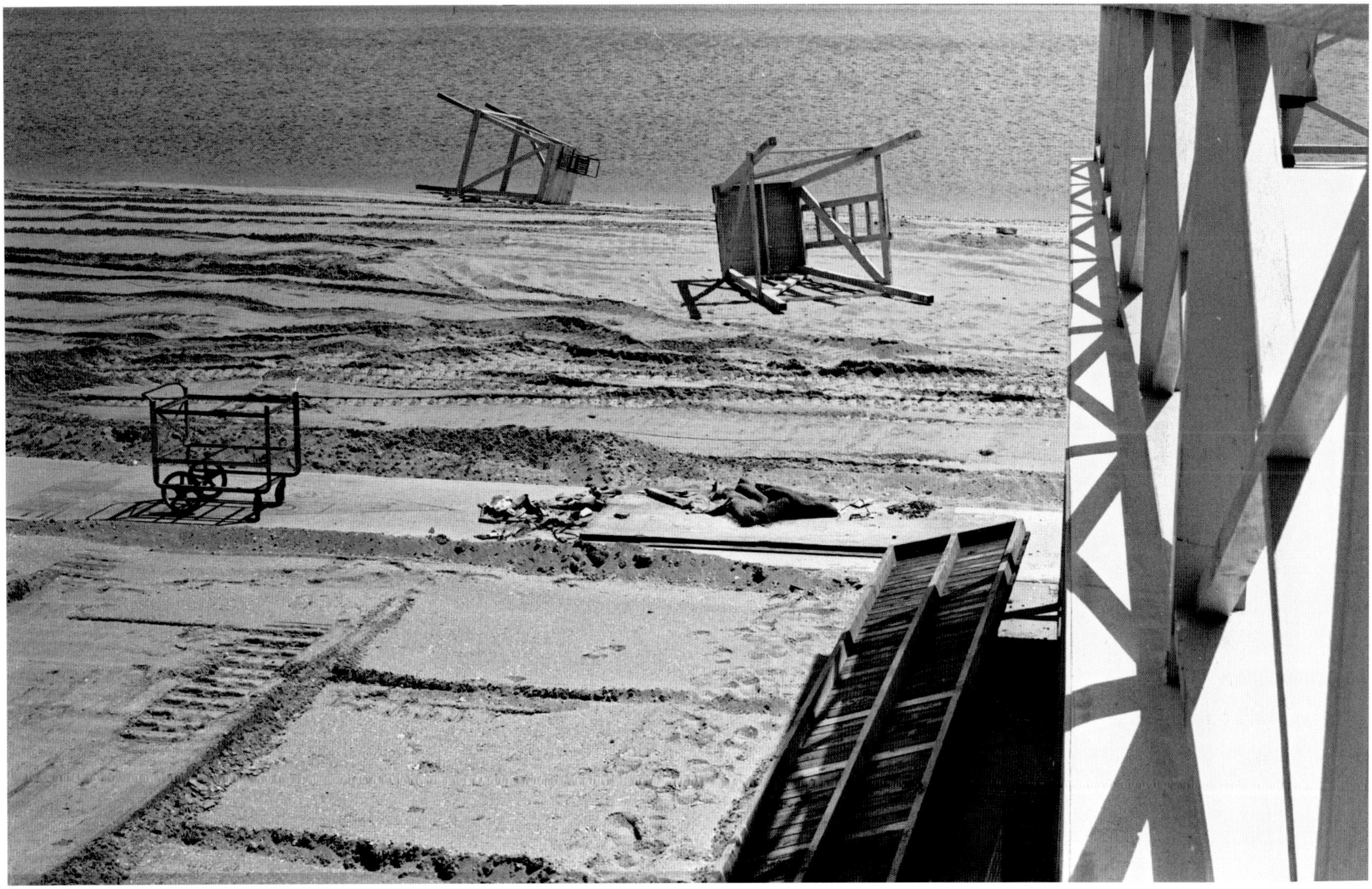

20

Fun House, Savin Rock, New Haven, Connecticut, 1958

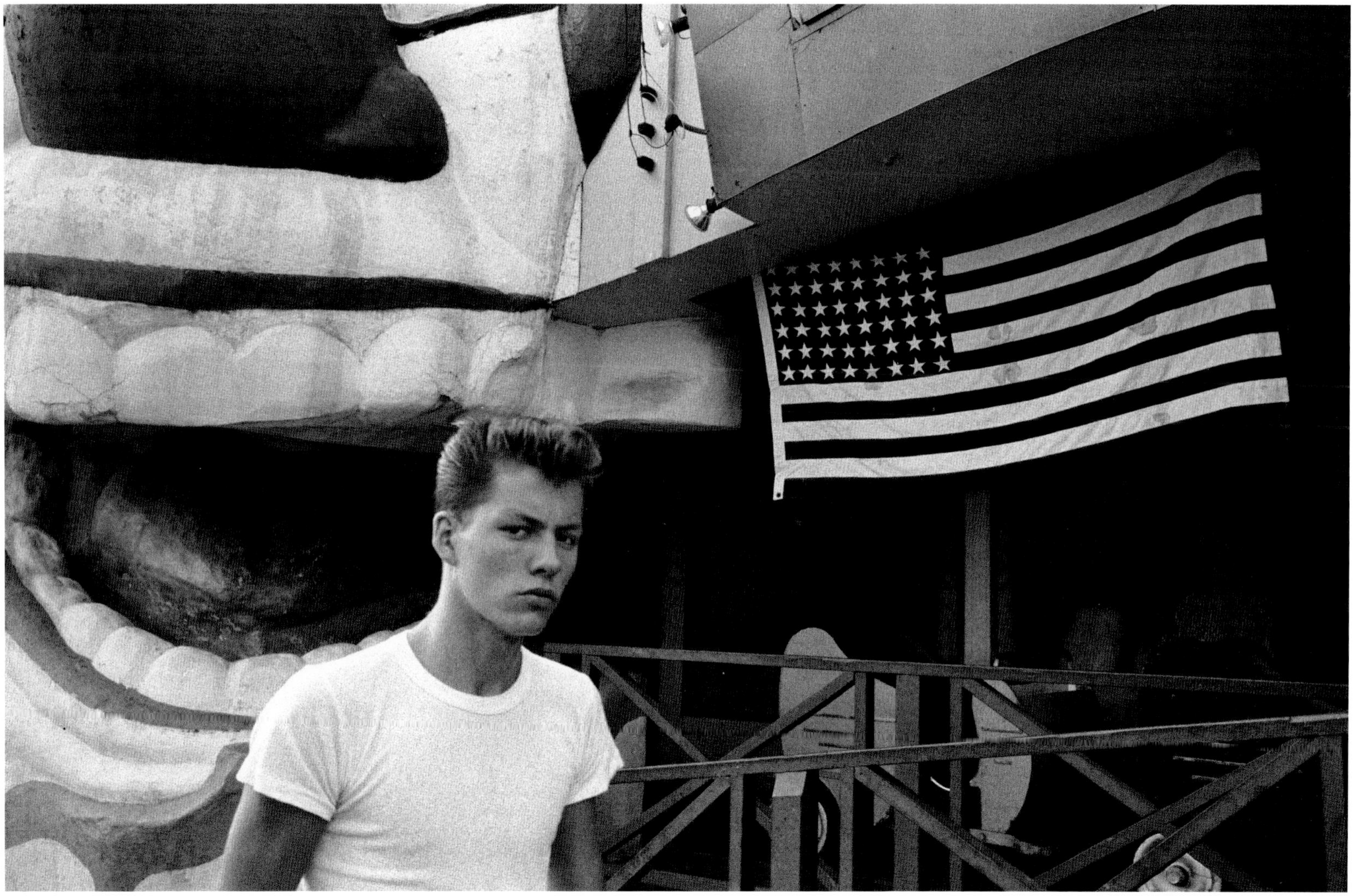

22

Reflections, New York, Park Avenue South, 1958

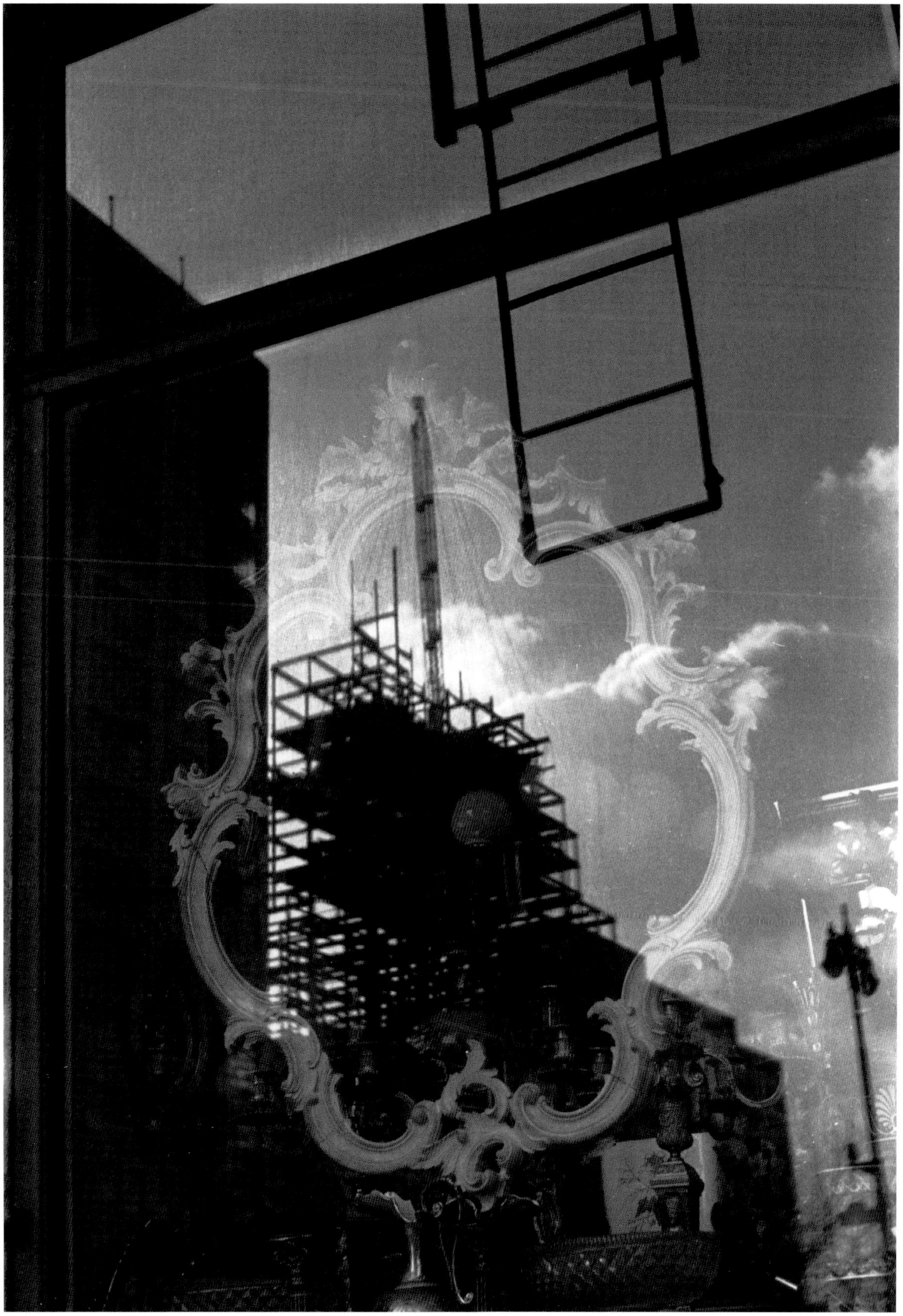

24

Horn & Hardart Automat, December 25, 1958

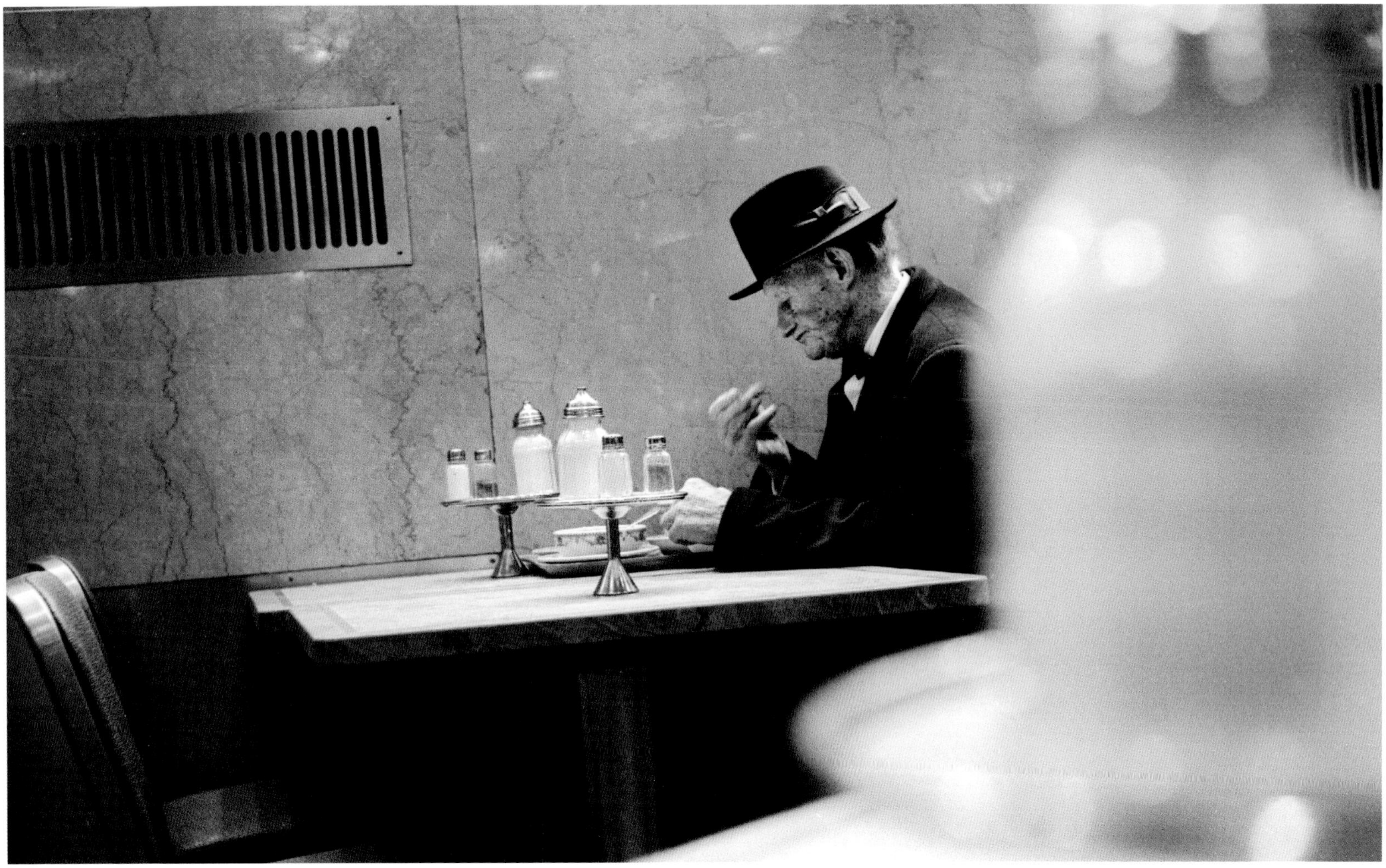

26

Horn & Hardart Automat, December, 1958

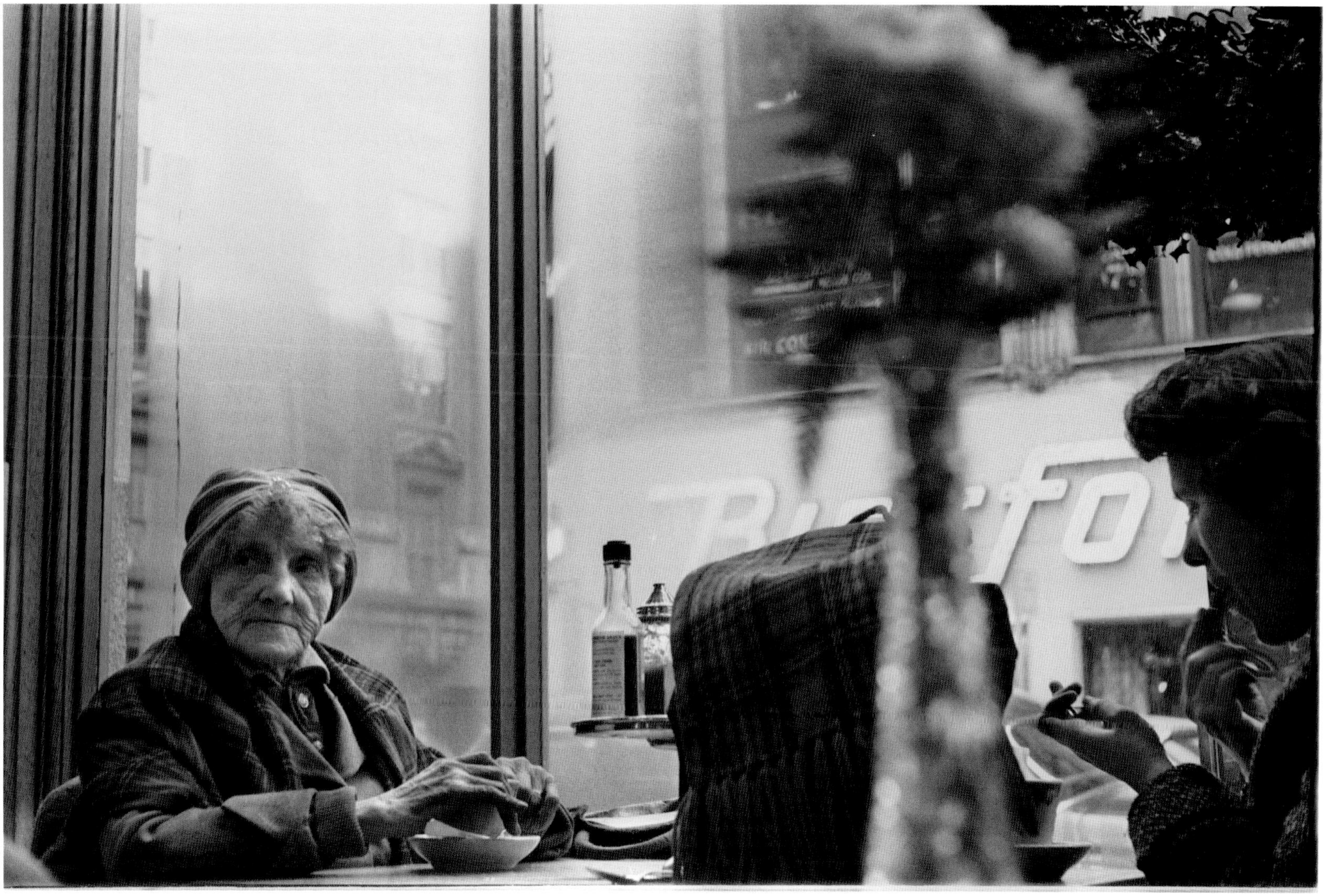

28

Anemone, Park Avenue South at East 40th Street, New York, 1958

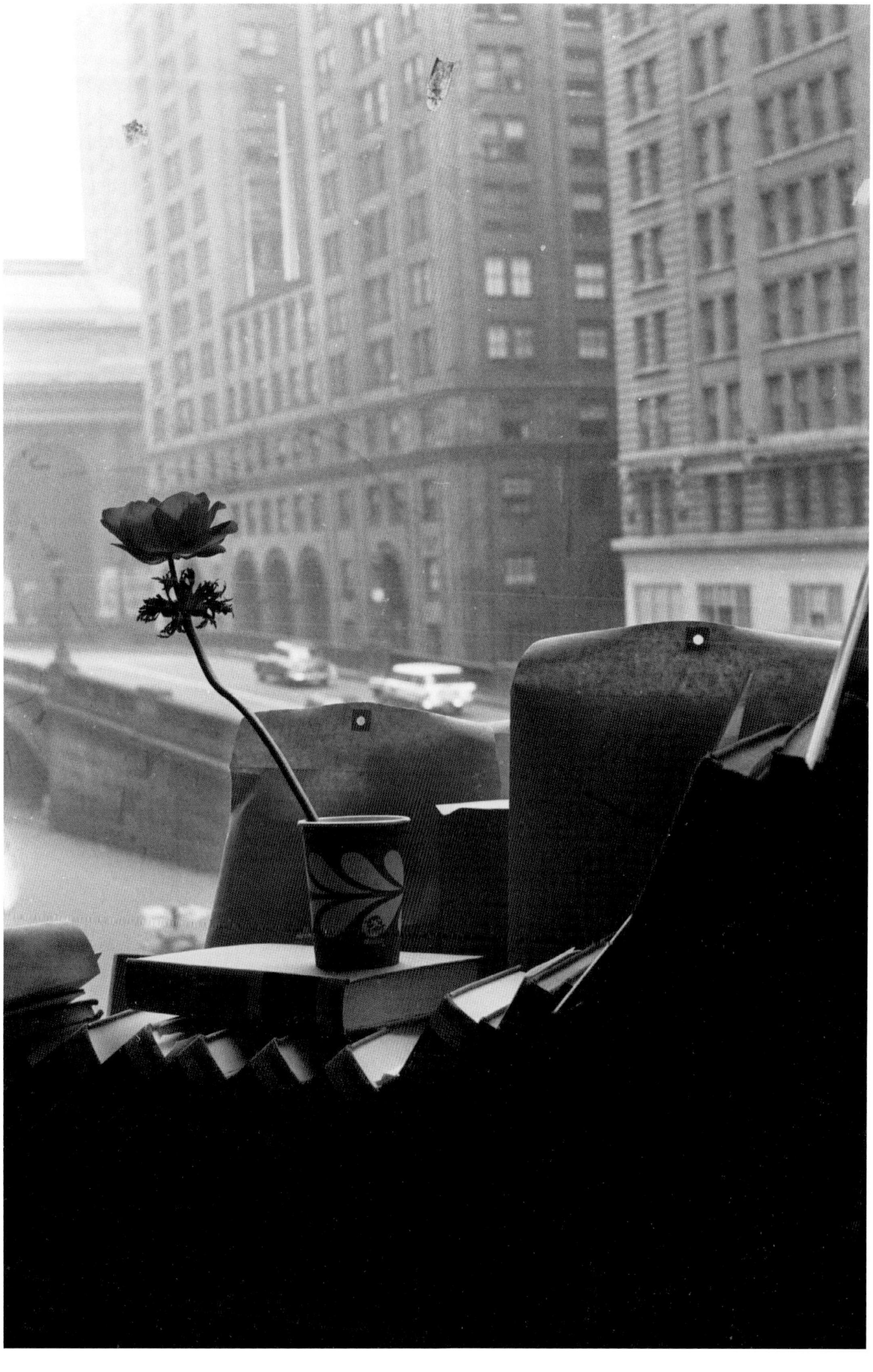

30

Park Avenue South at East 40th Street, New York, 1958

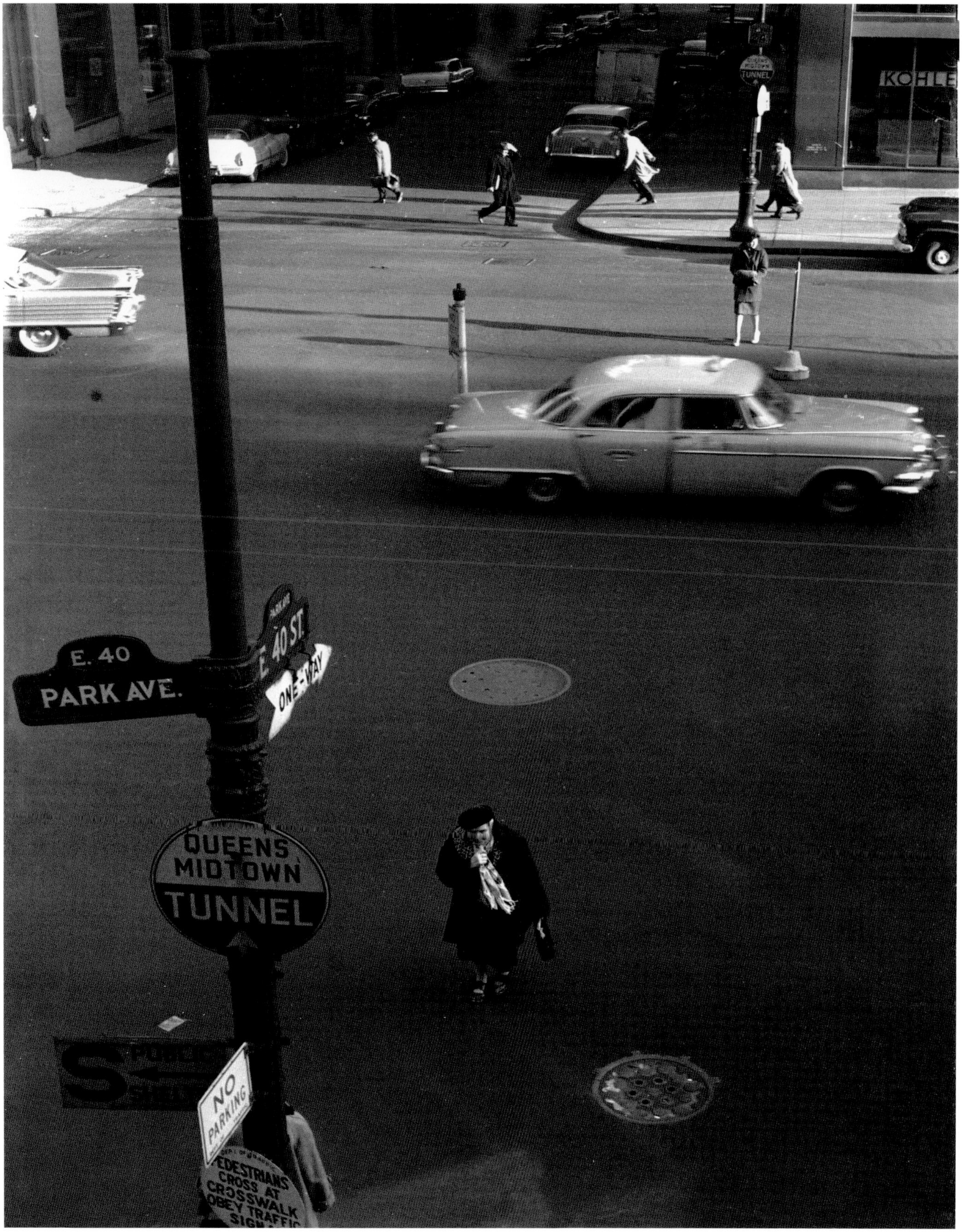
E. 40
PARK AVE.
E. 40 ST.
QUEENS
MIDTOWN
TUNNEL
NO
PARKING
CROSS AT
CROSSWALK
OBEY TRAFFIC

32

Empire State Building, New York, 1983

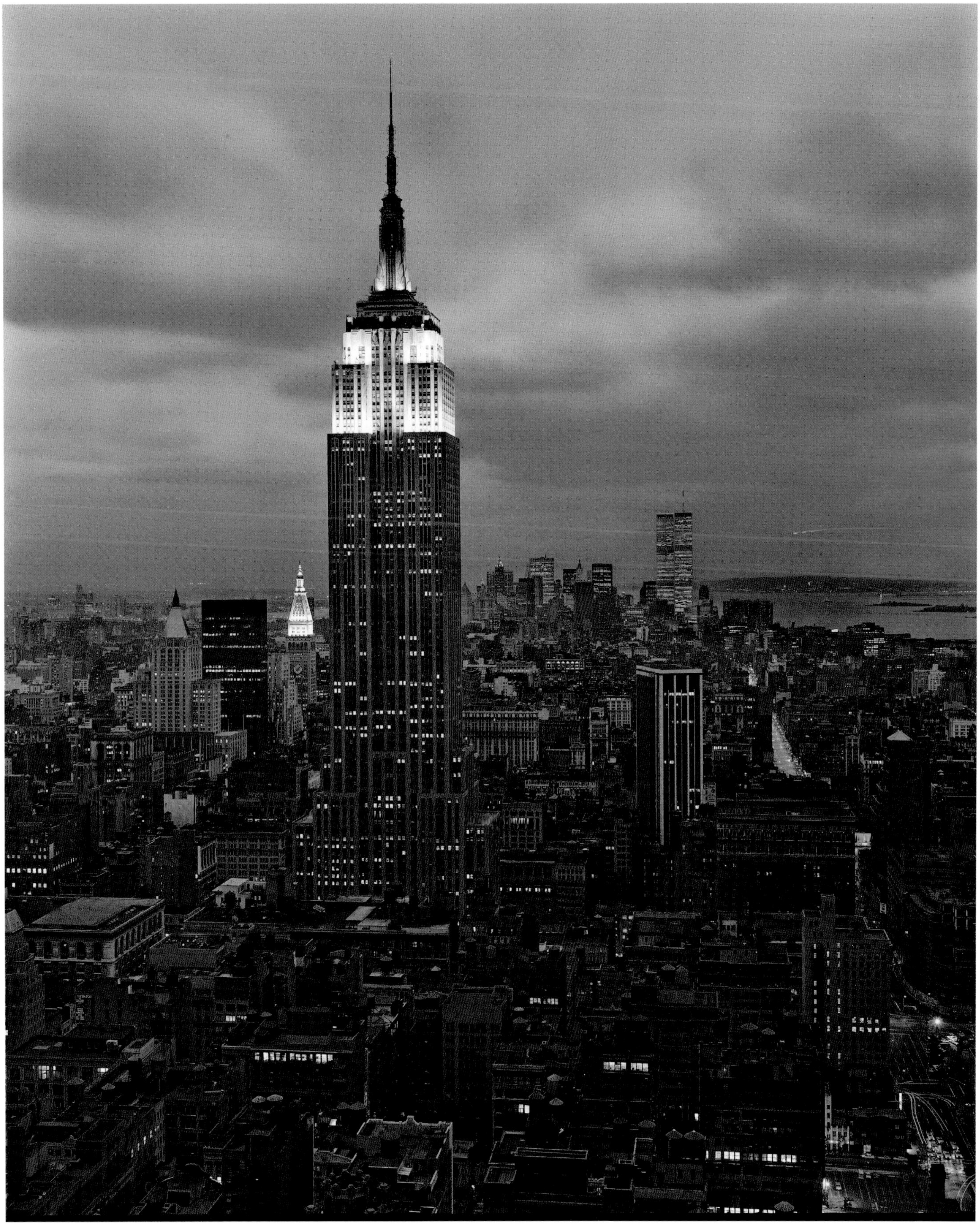

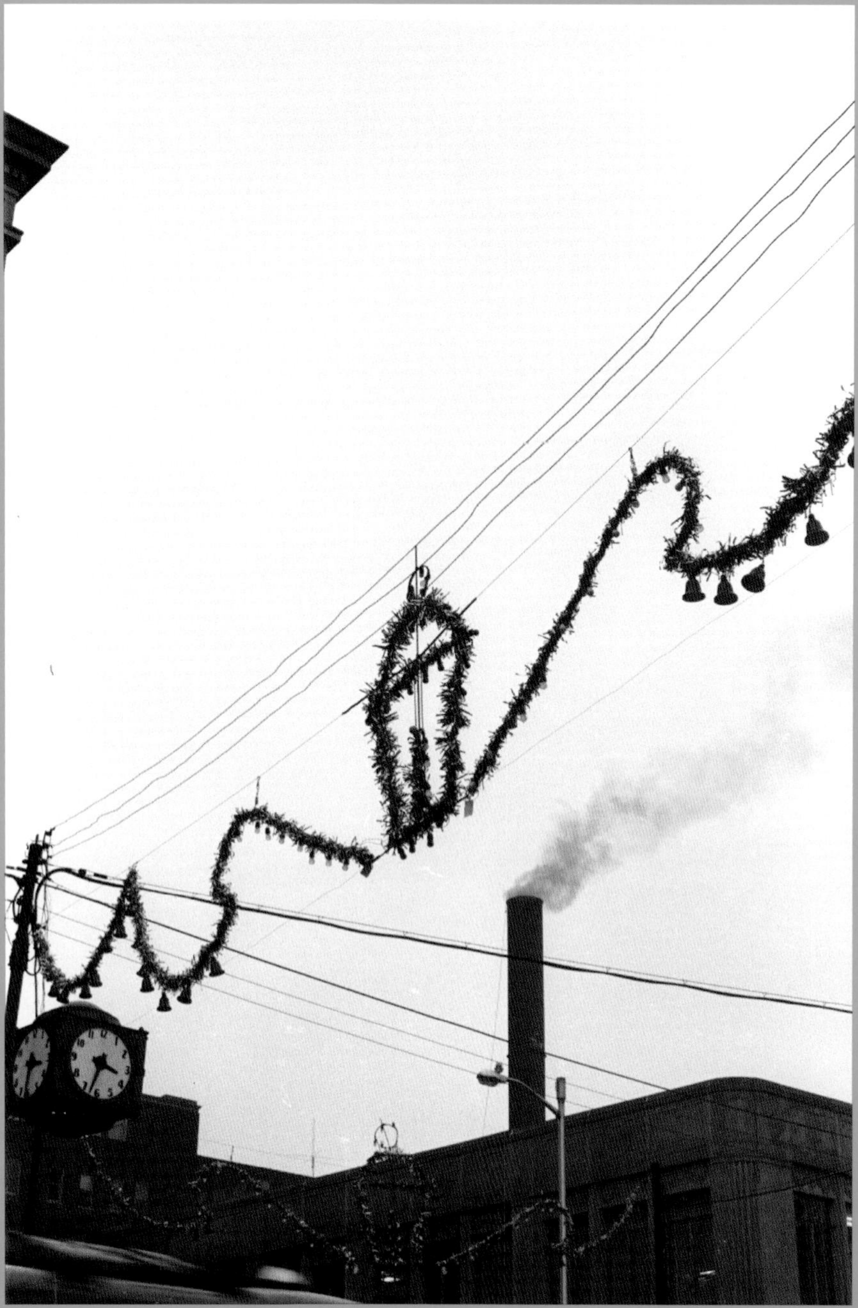

Intersection of Temple and Chapel Streets, New Haven, Connecticut, 1958

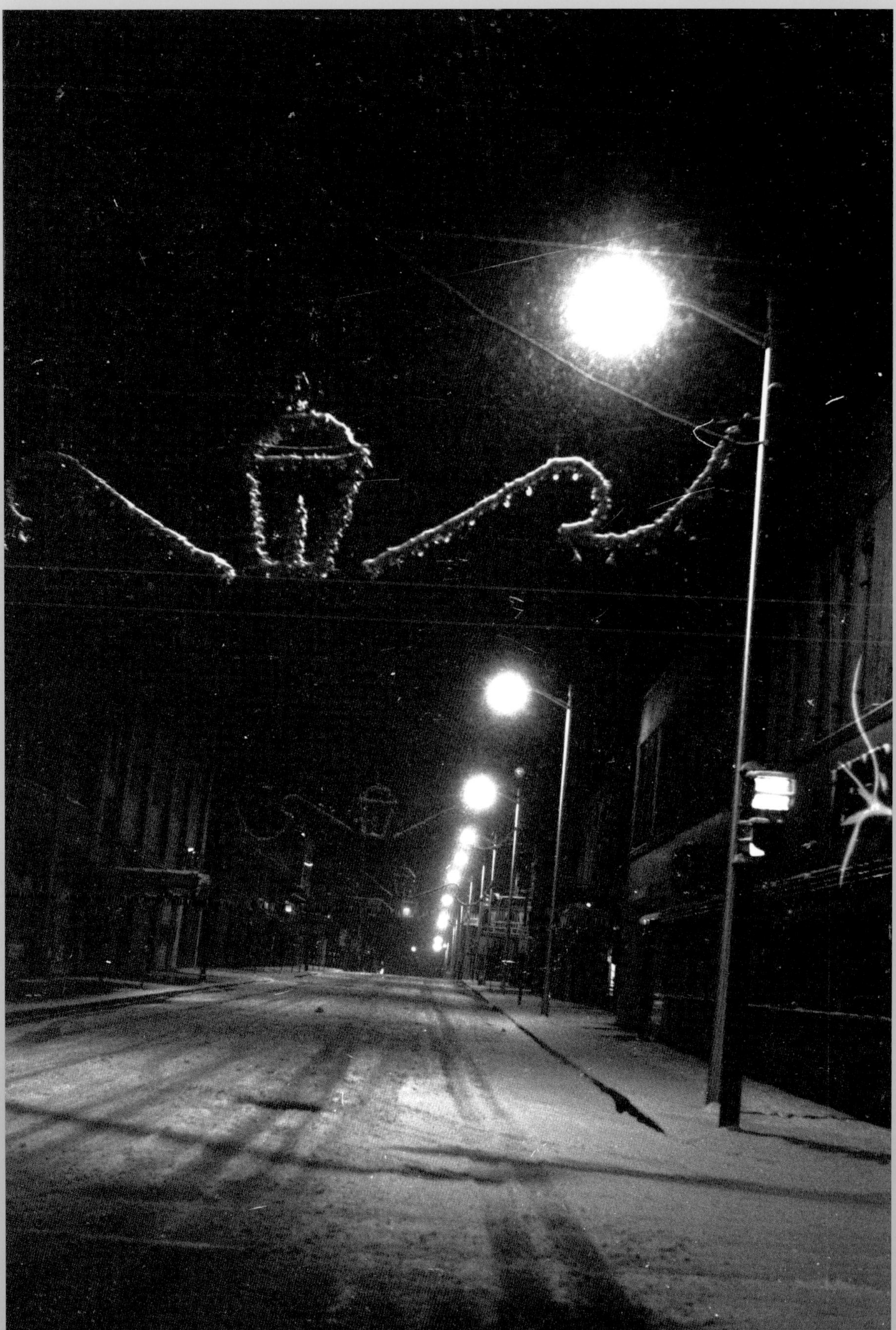

36

Dorothy O'Connor, New Haven, Connecticut, 1958

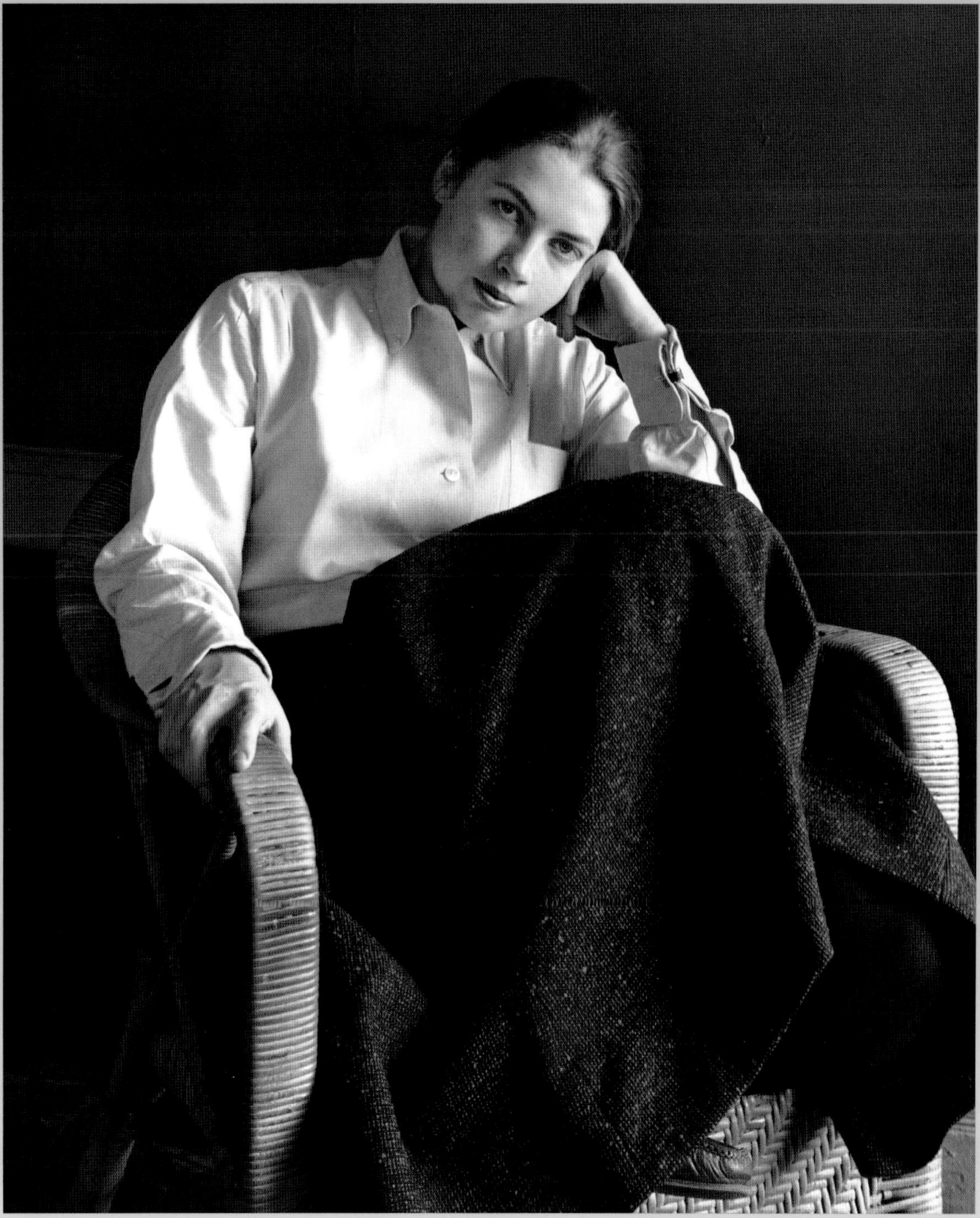

São Paulo, Brazil, 1958

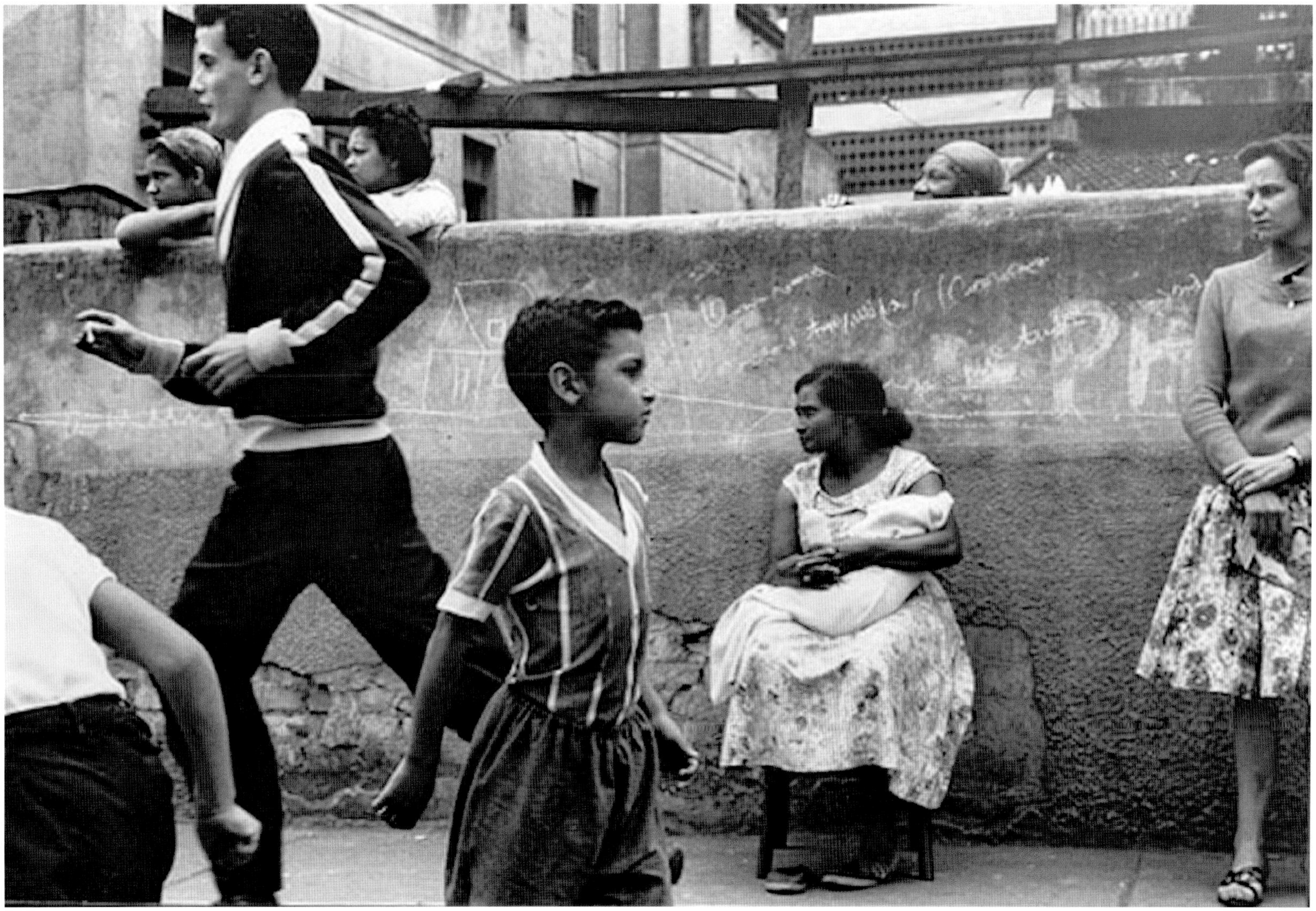

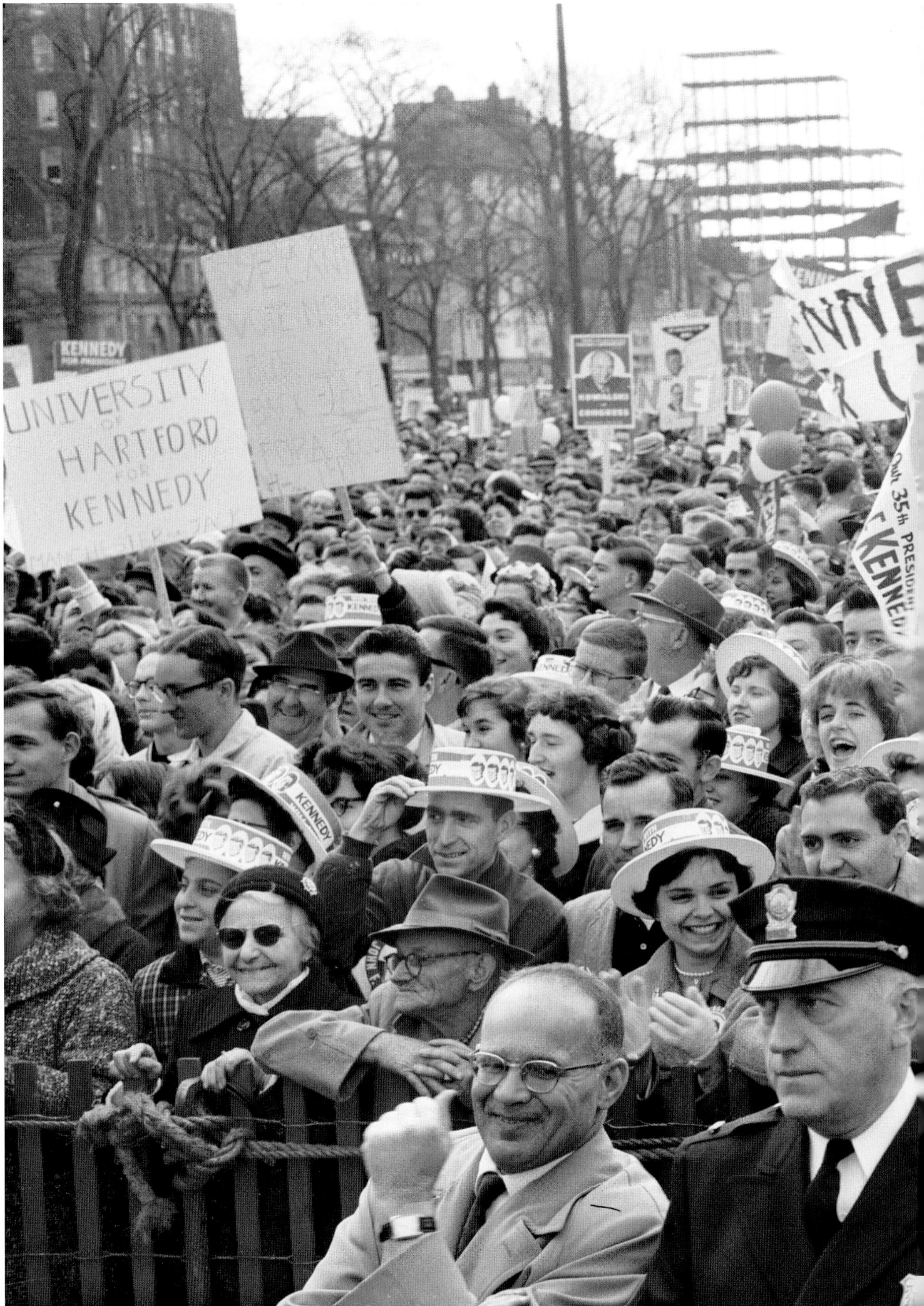

Kennedy Rally,
New Haven Green,
September, 1960

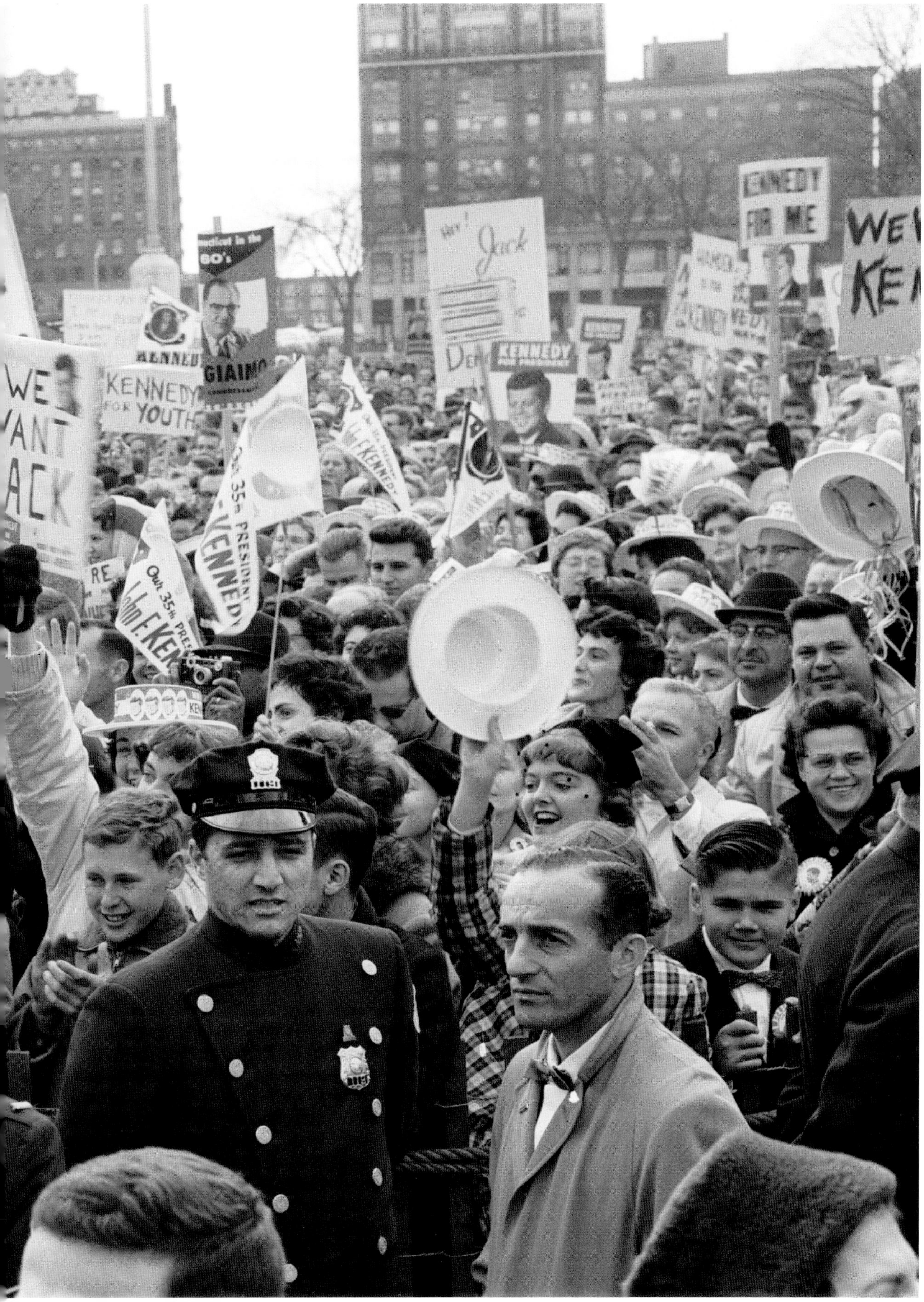
KENNEDY FOR ME
Hey! Jack
KENNEDY
KENNEDY FOR YOUTH
GIAIMO
Our 35th PRESIDENT

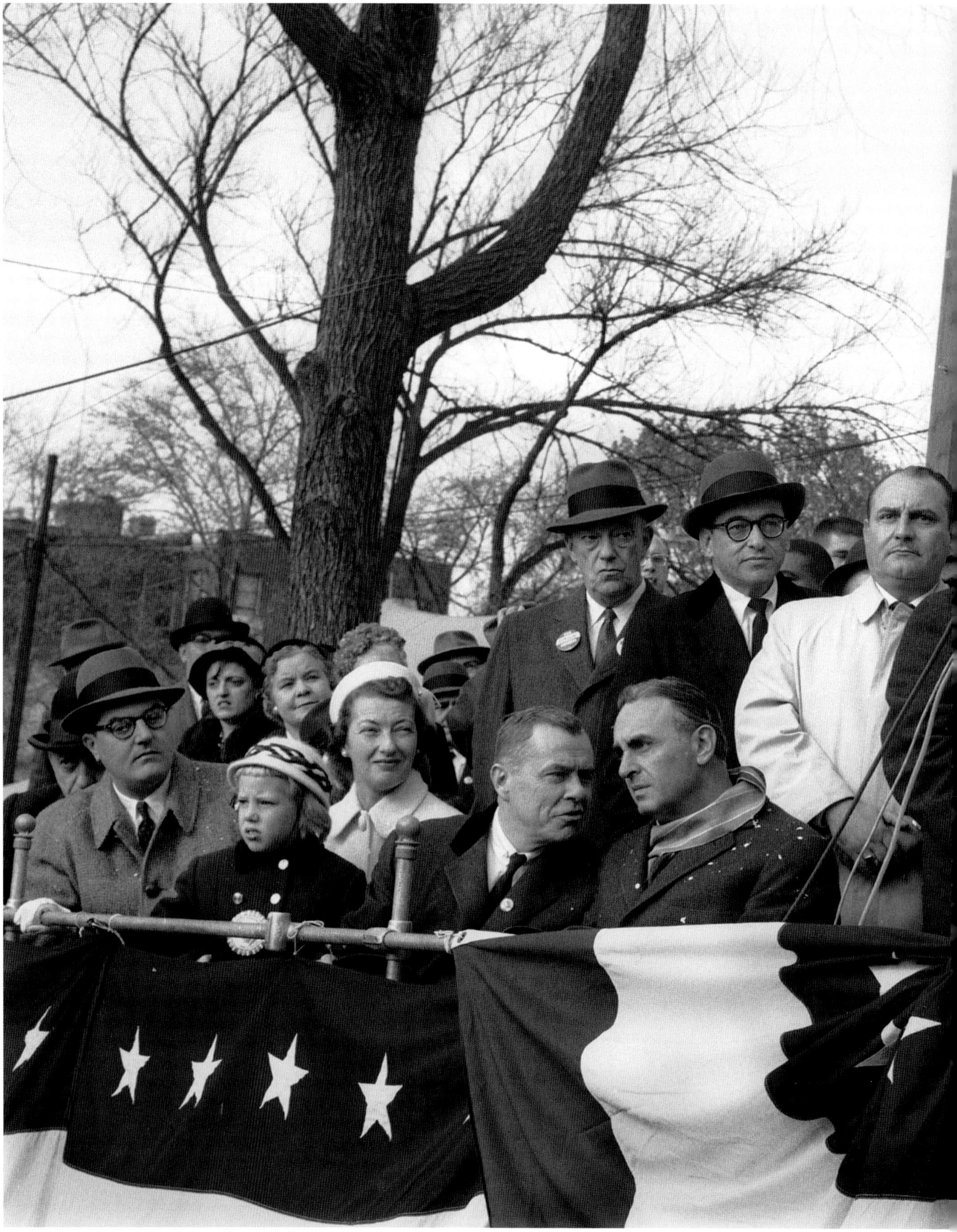

Kennedy Rally,
New Haven Green,
September, 1960

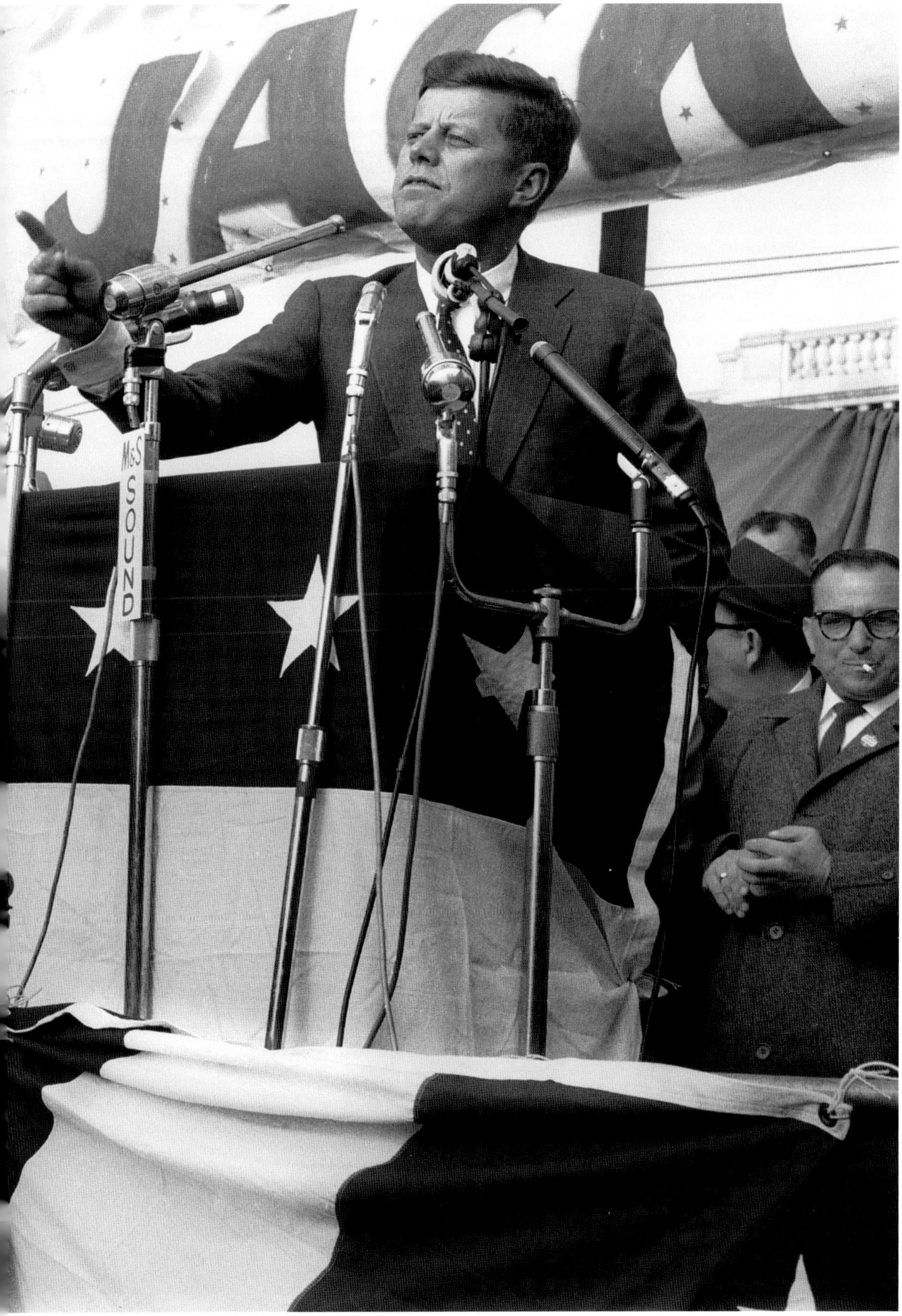
M&S SOUND

44

Souvenir Shop Facing St. Peter's Square, Rome, Italy, 1964

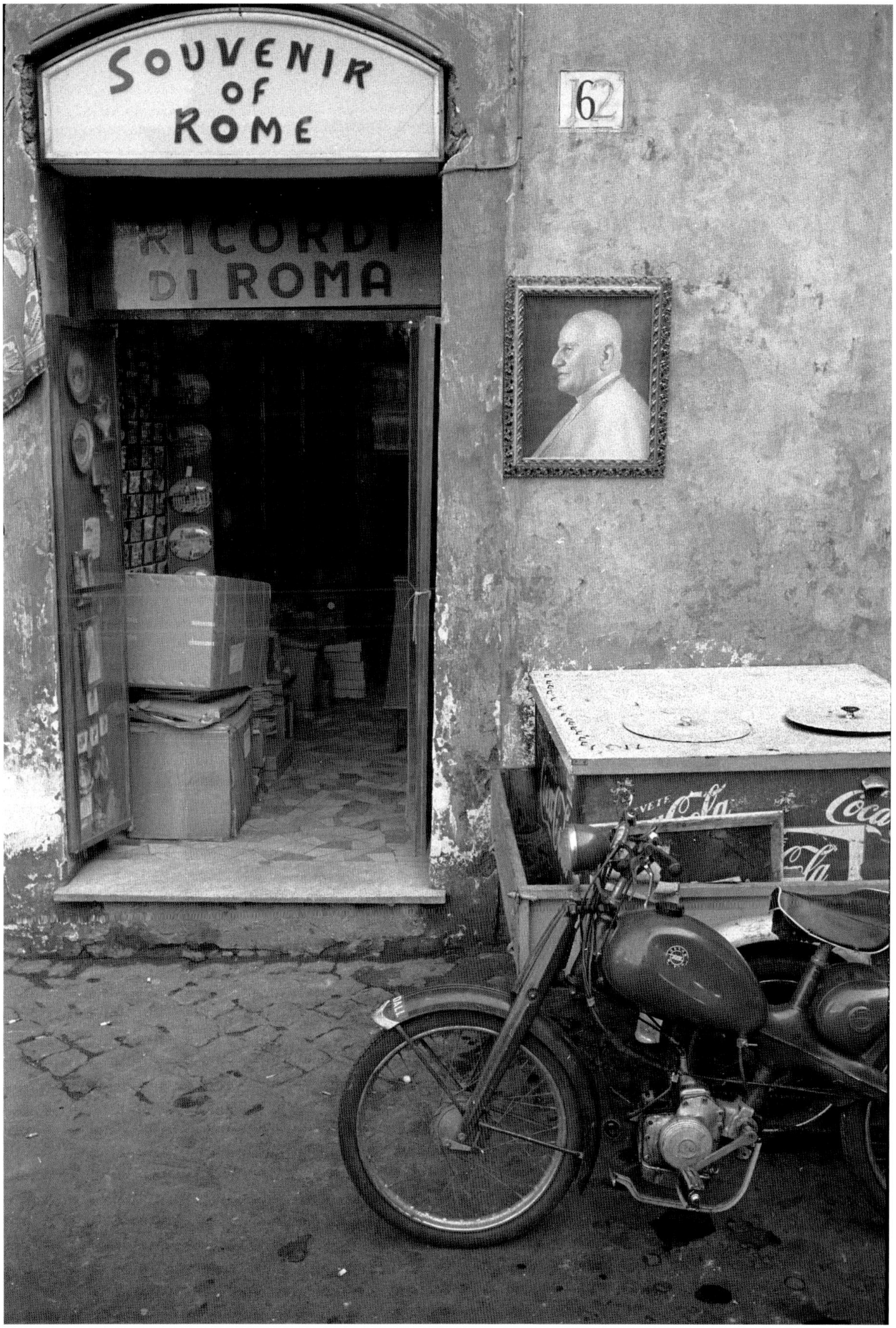
SOUVENIR
OF
ROME
62
RICORDI
DI ROMA

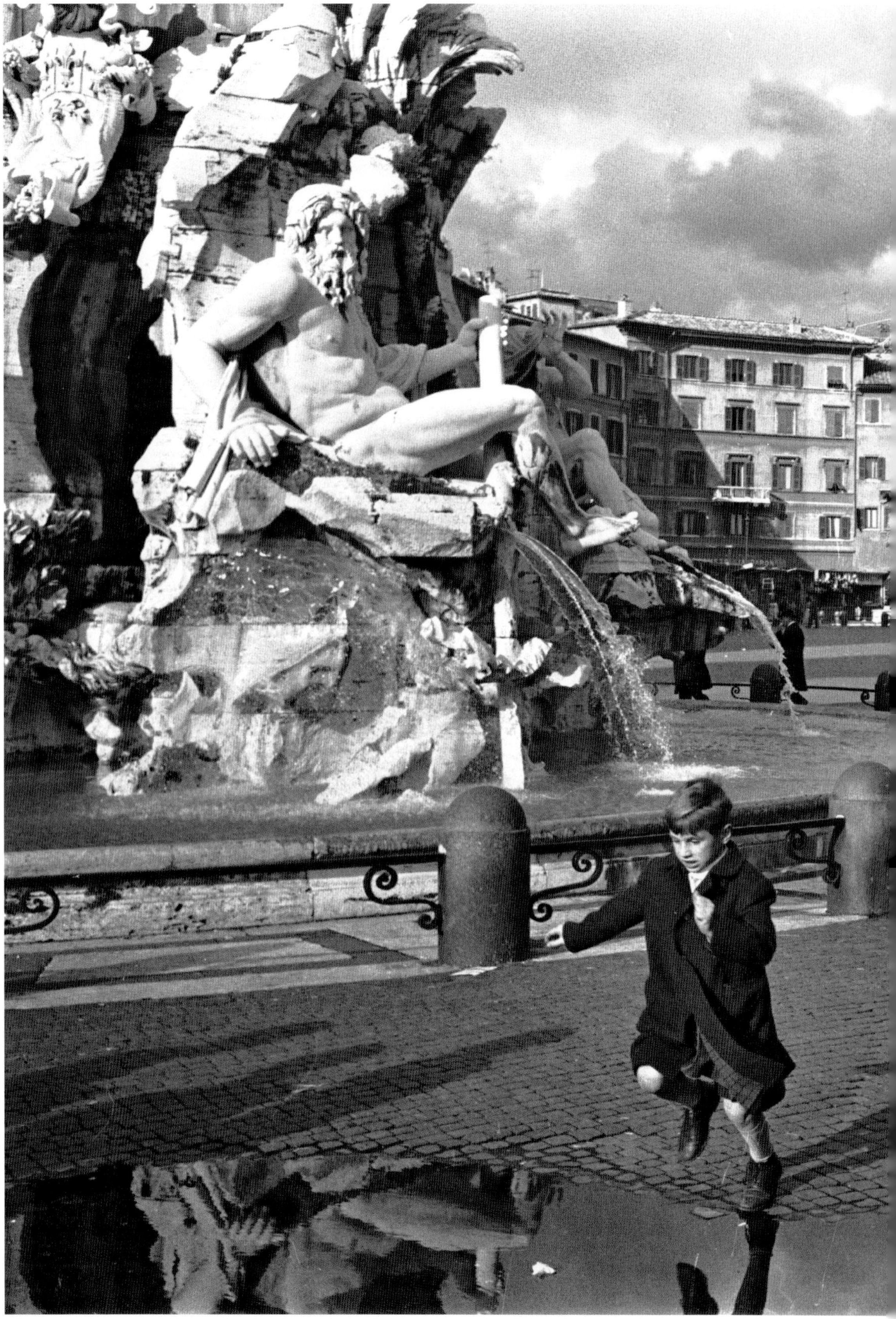

Piazza Navona, Rome
December, 1964

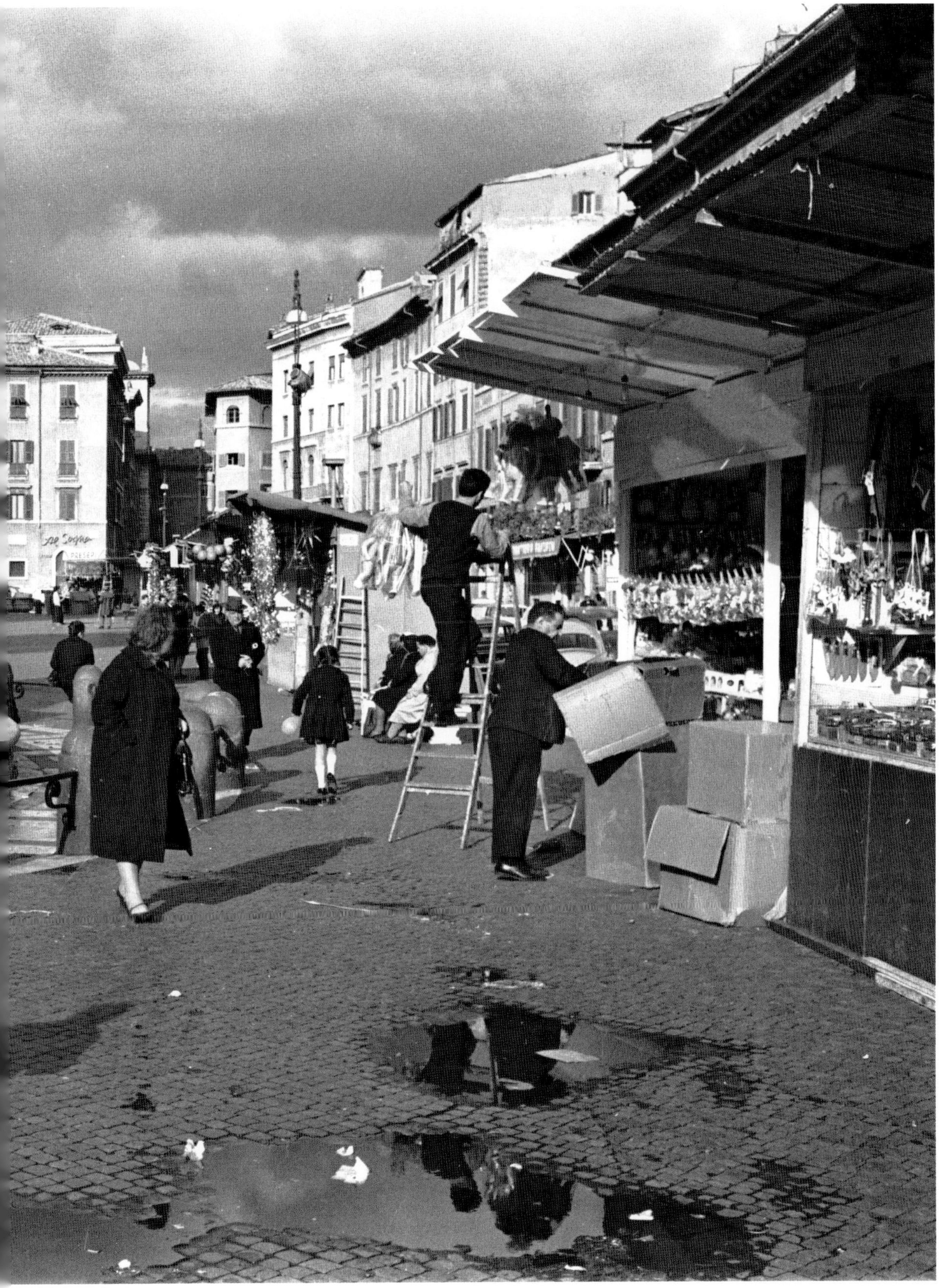

Anzio Beach, Suburban Rome, Italy, 1964

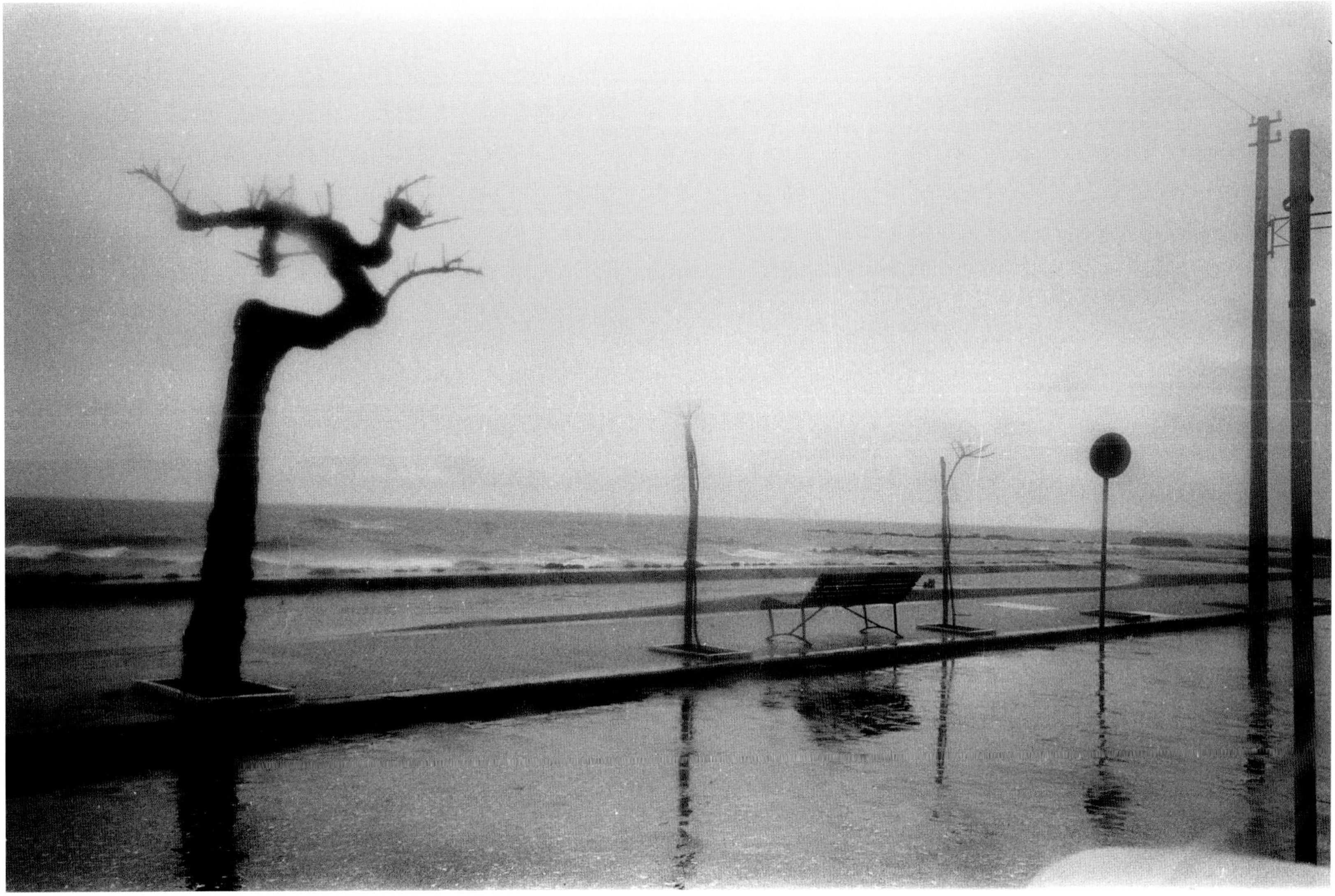

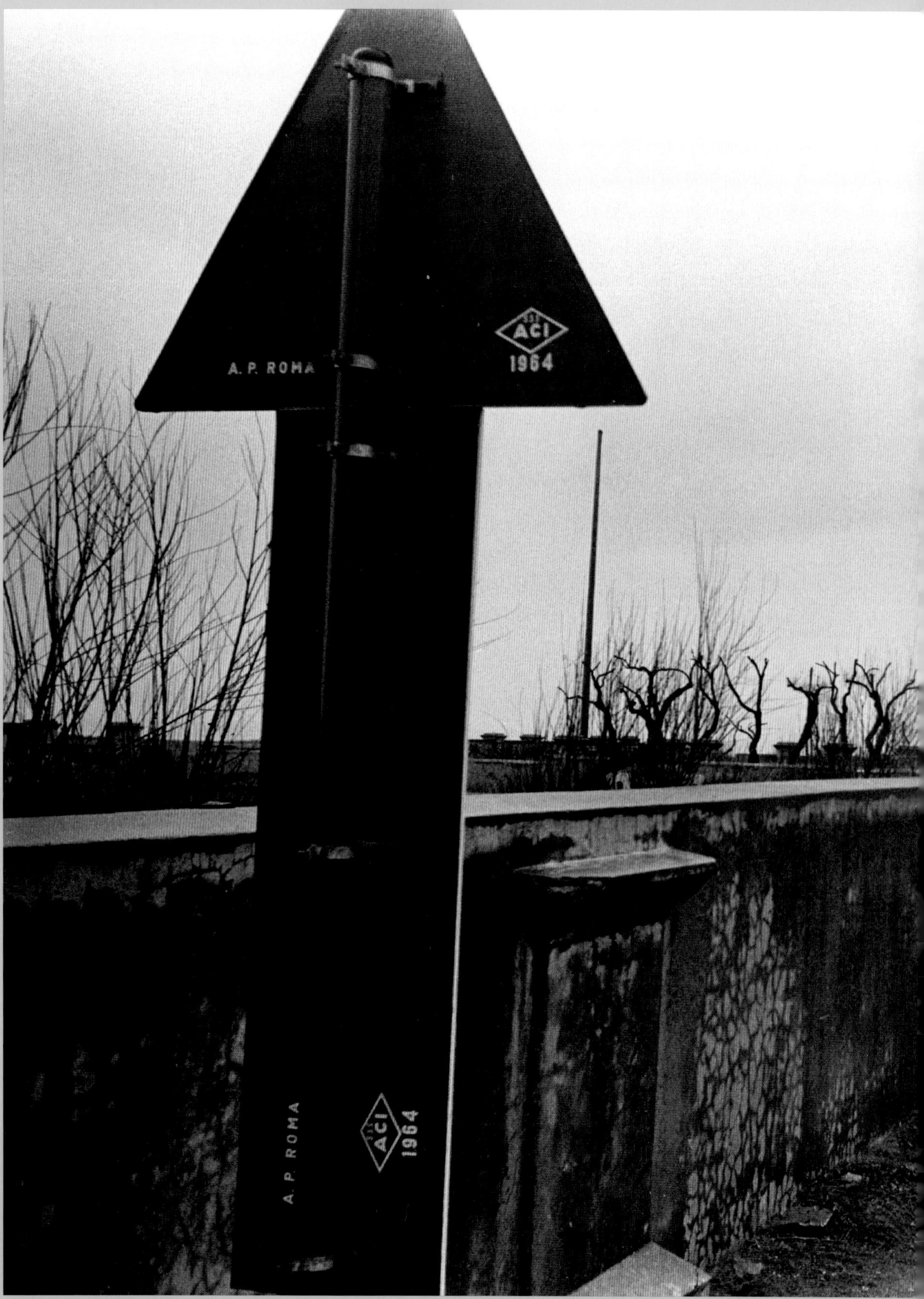
A. P. ROMA
ACI
1964
A. P. ROMA
ACI
1964

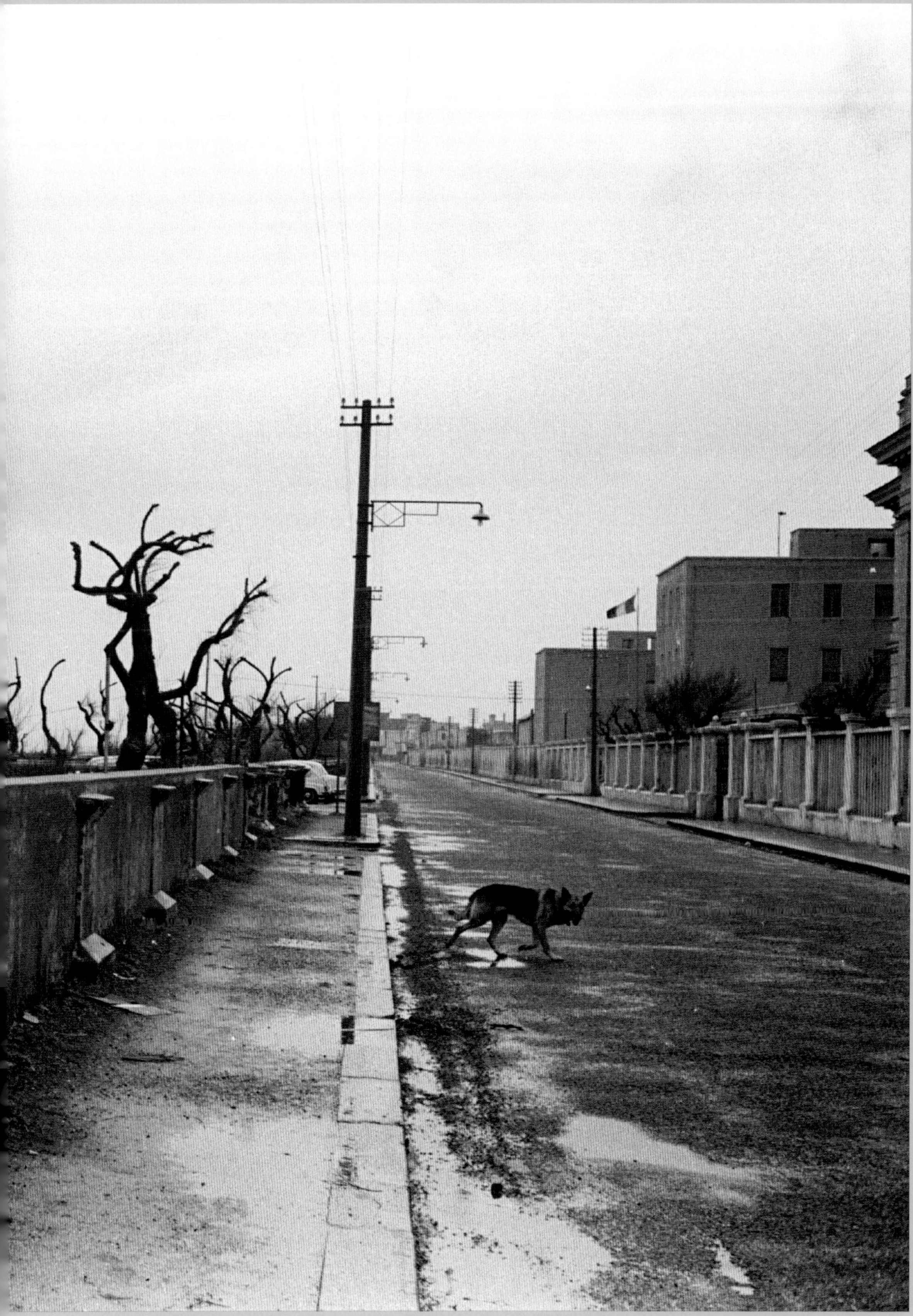

Parallel to Anzio Beach
Italy, 1964

52

Malibu Beach, California, ca. 1960

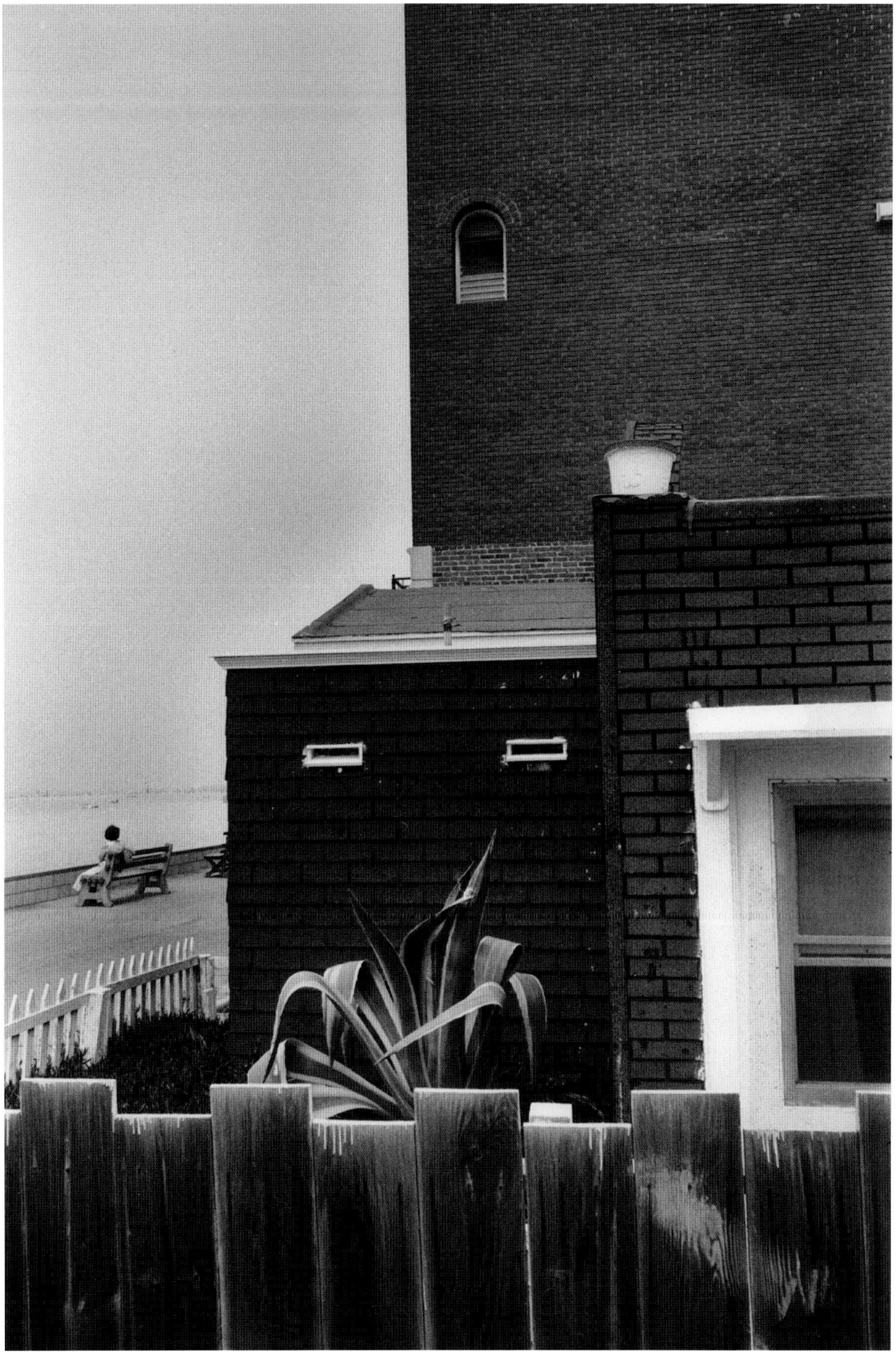

54

Santa Monica, California, ca. 1960

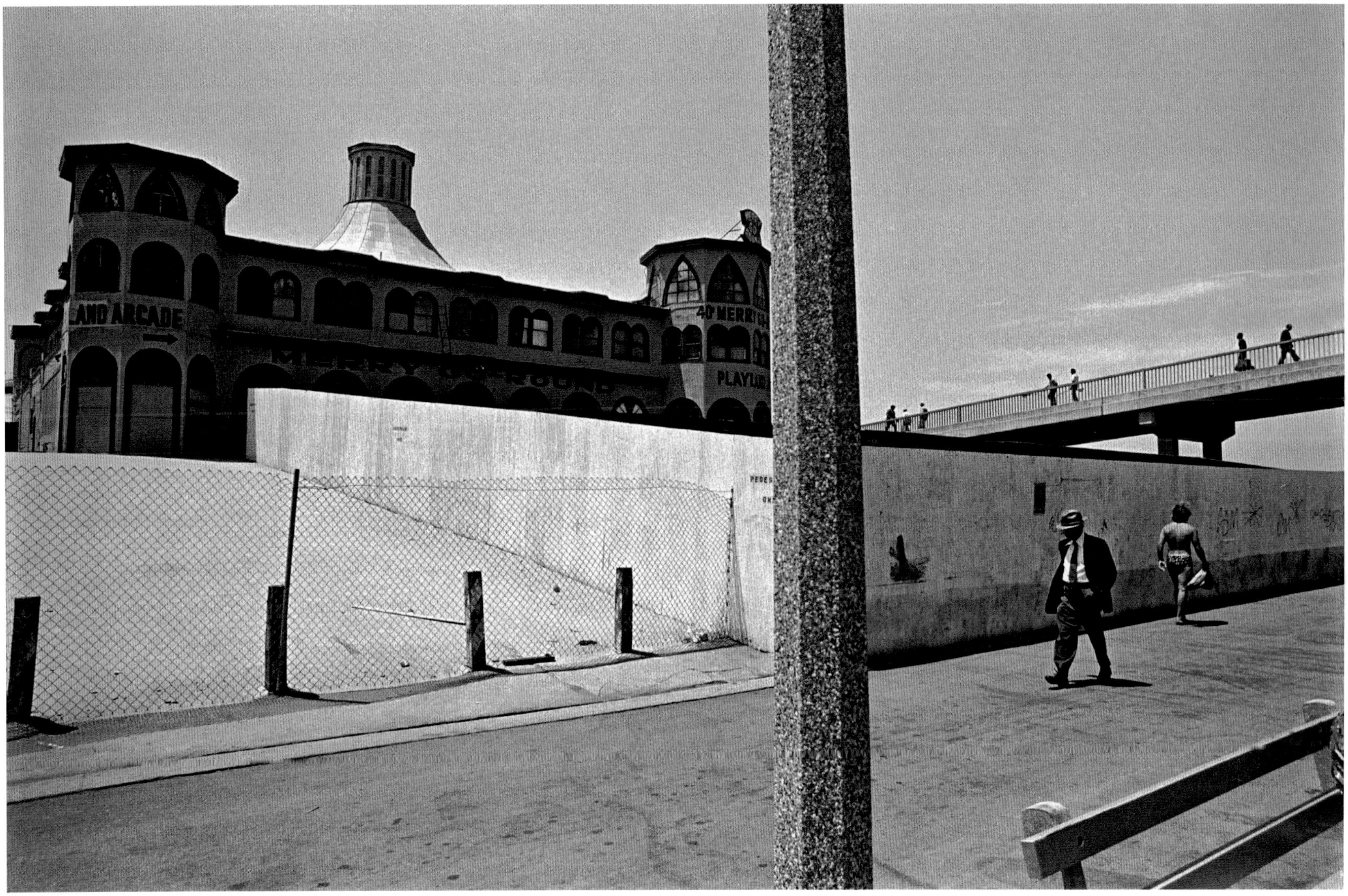
LAND ARCADE

Santa Monica Boardwalk, California, ca. 1960

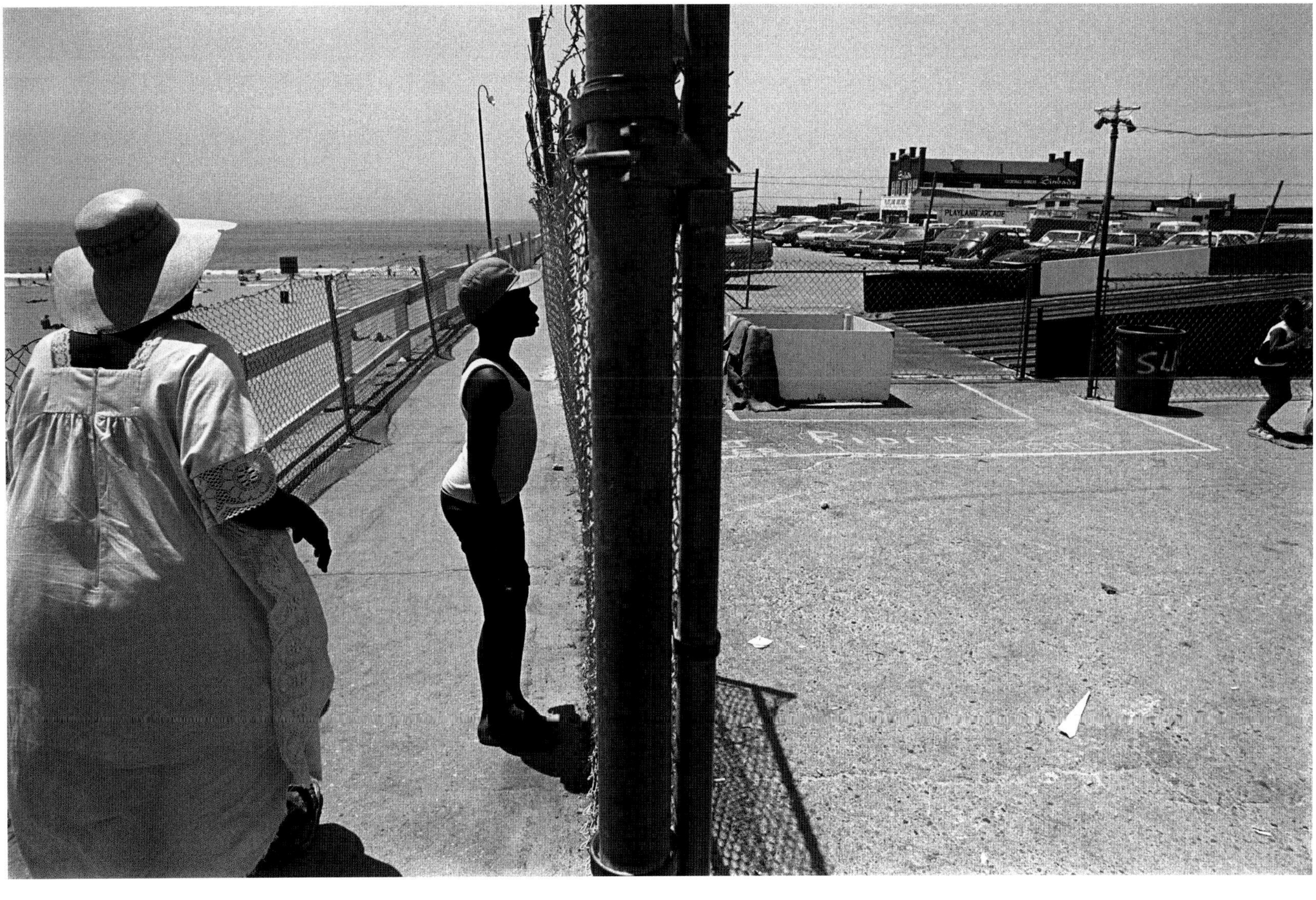
PLAYLAND ARCADE

58

Maysville, Georgia, ca. 1963

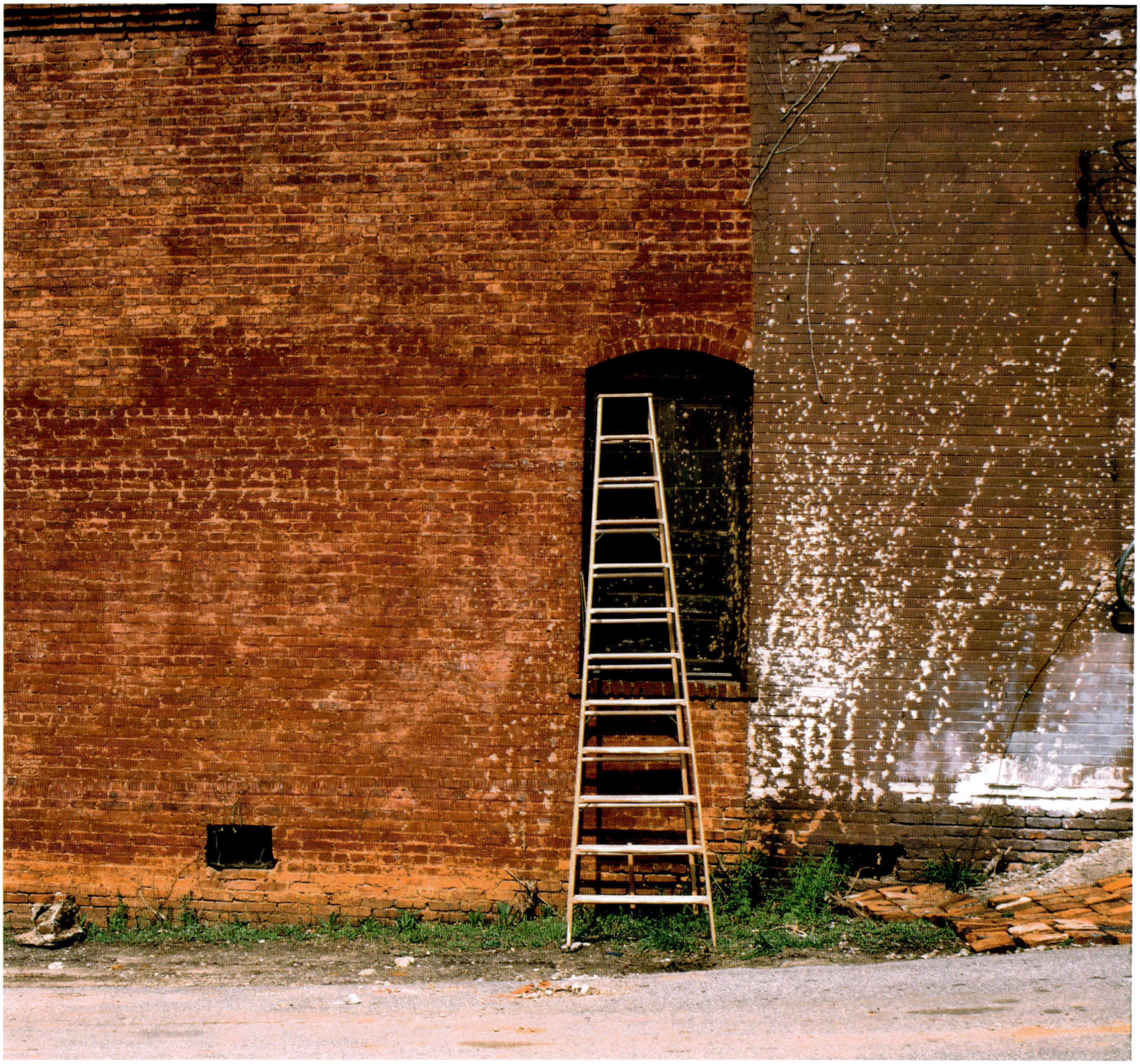

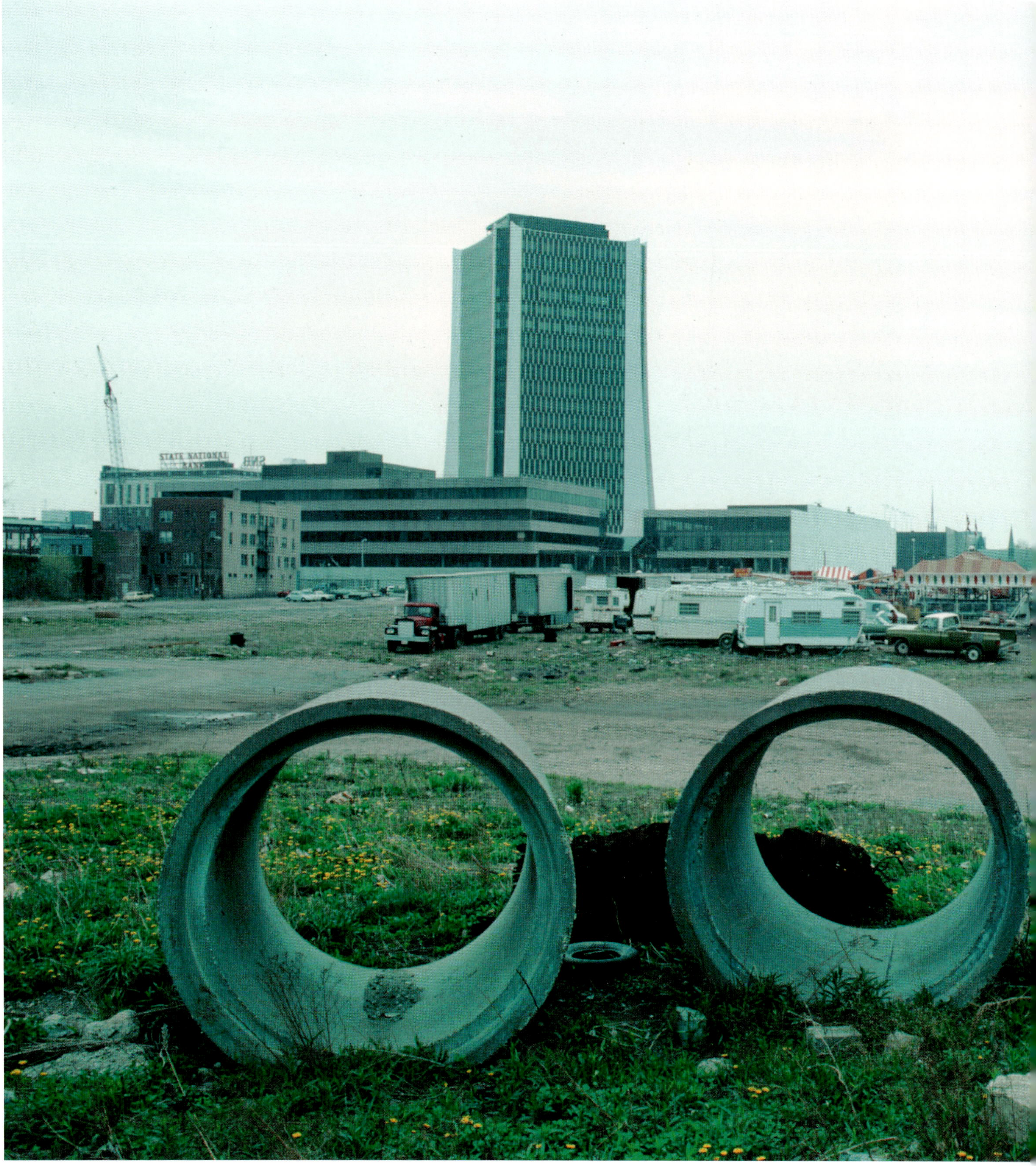
STATE NATIONAL
BANK

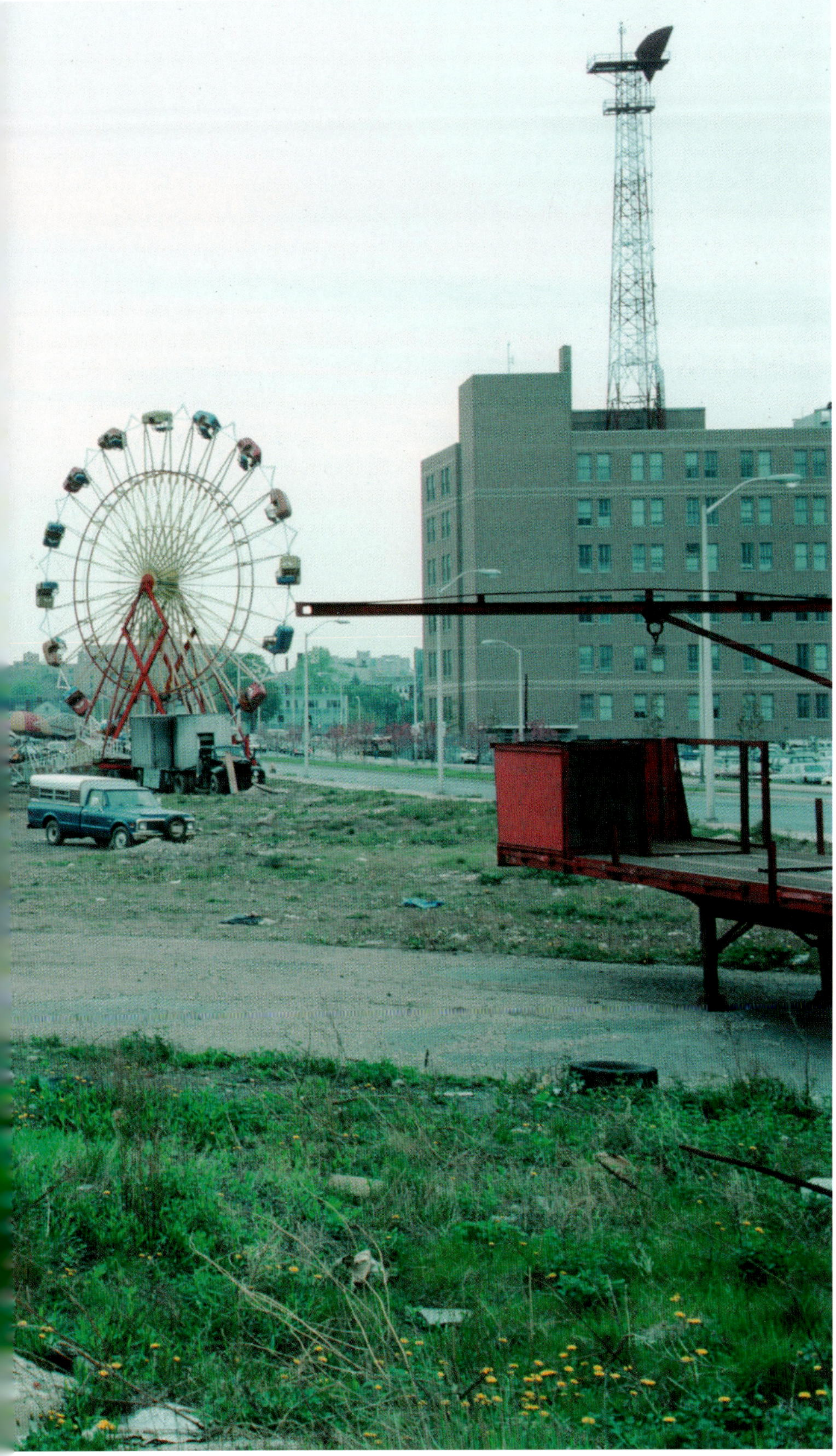

Stamford, Connecticut, ca. 1974

62

Taxi Interior, Queens, New York, ca. 1970

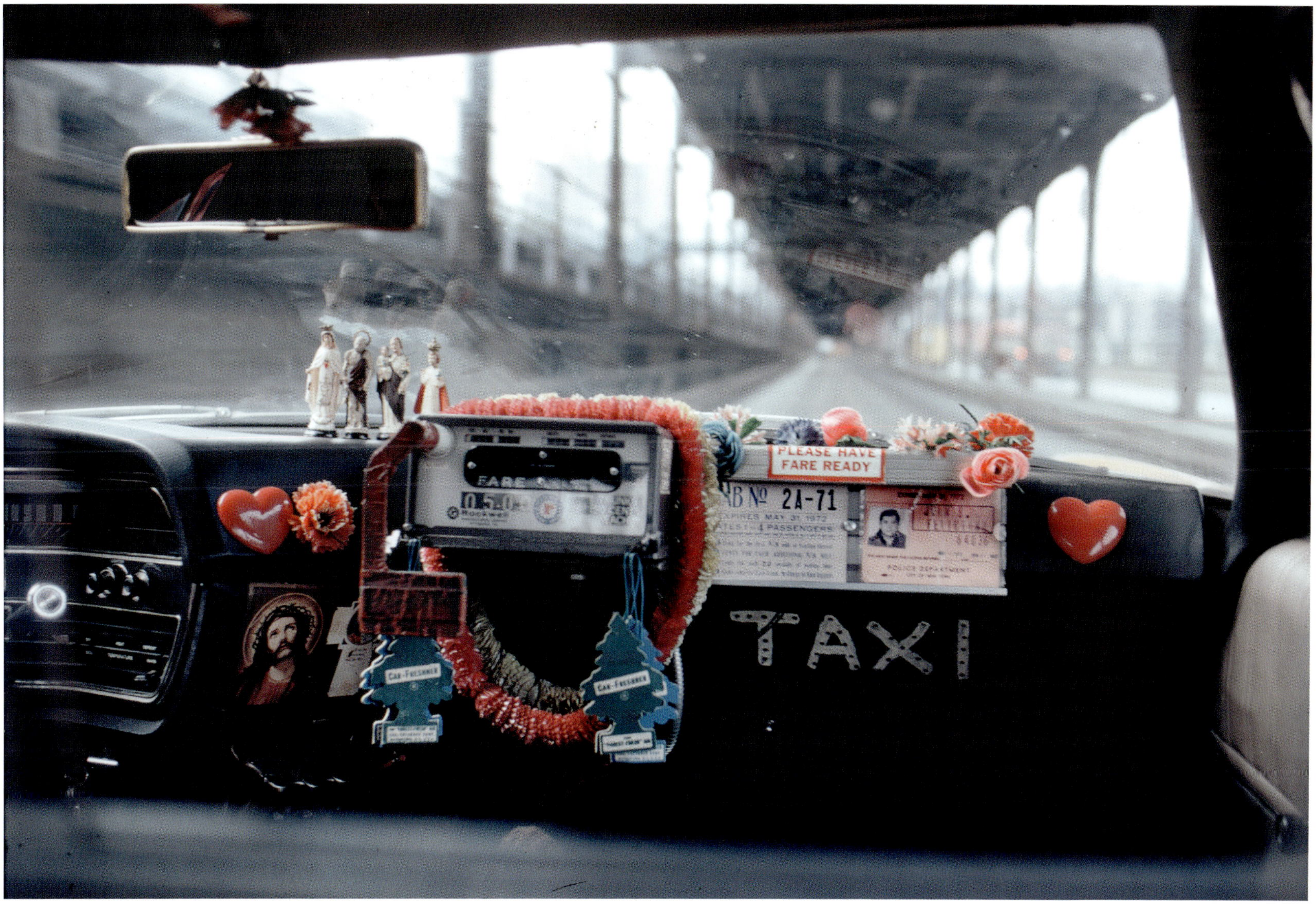
PLEASE HAVE
FARE READY
FARE
EXPIRES MAY 31, 1972
POLICE DEPARTMENT
TAXI

Tank Farm, Macintosh, Georgia, 1981

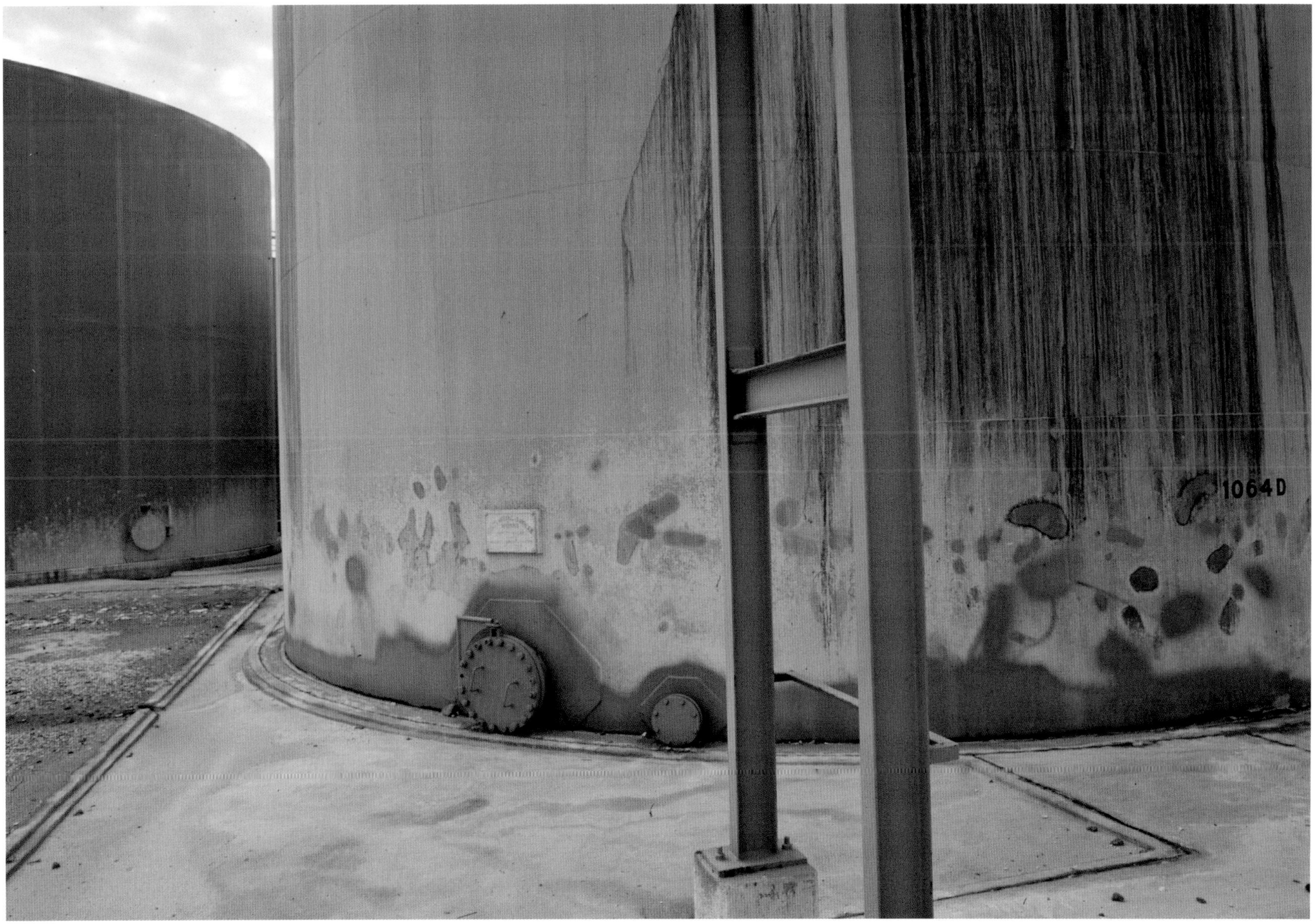
1064D

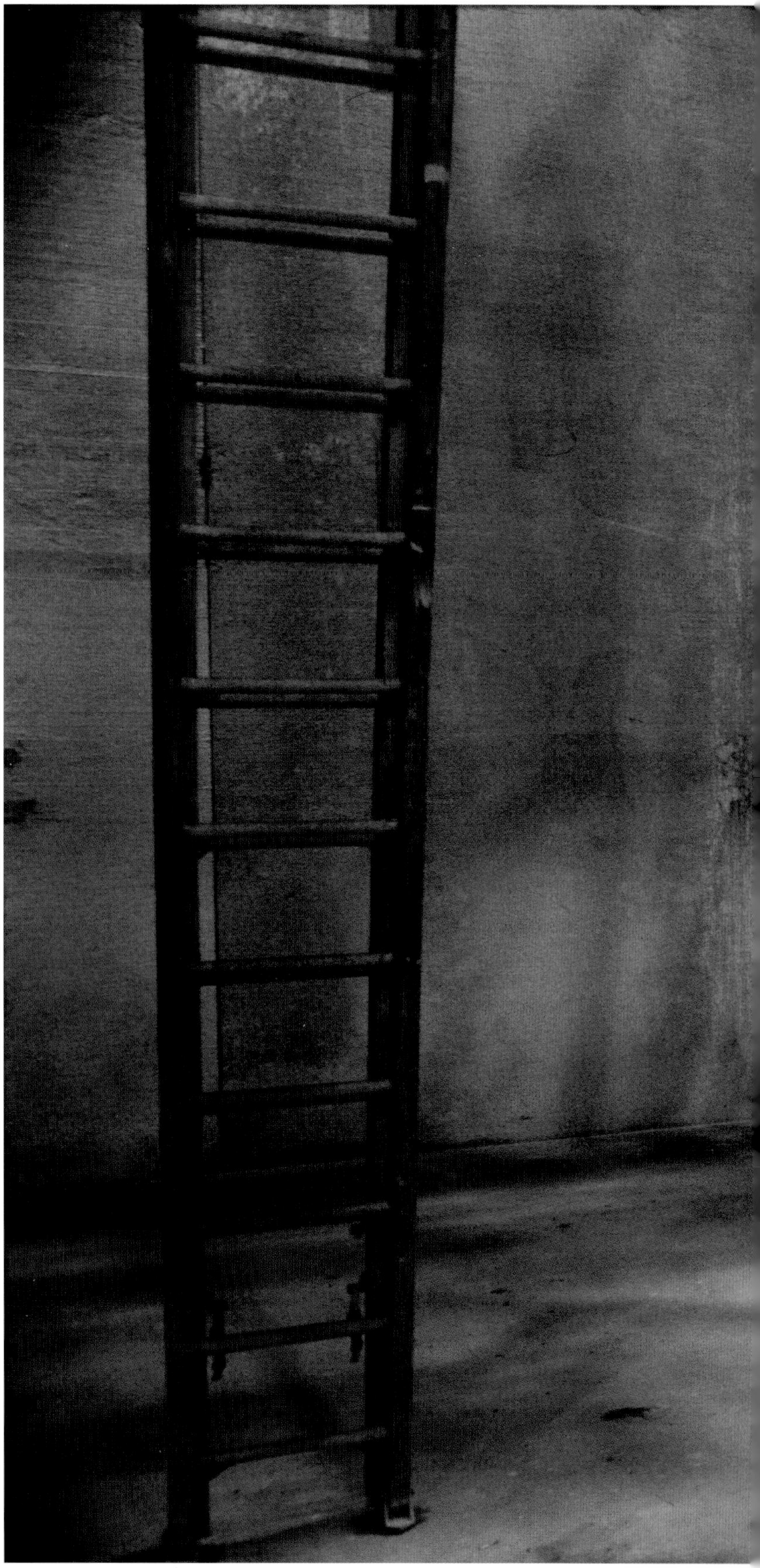

Industrial Interior, Macintosh, Georgia, 1981

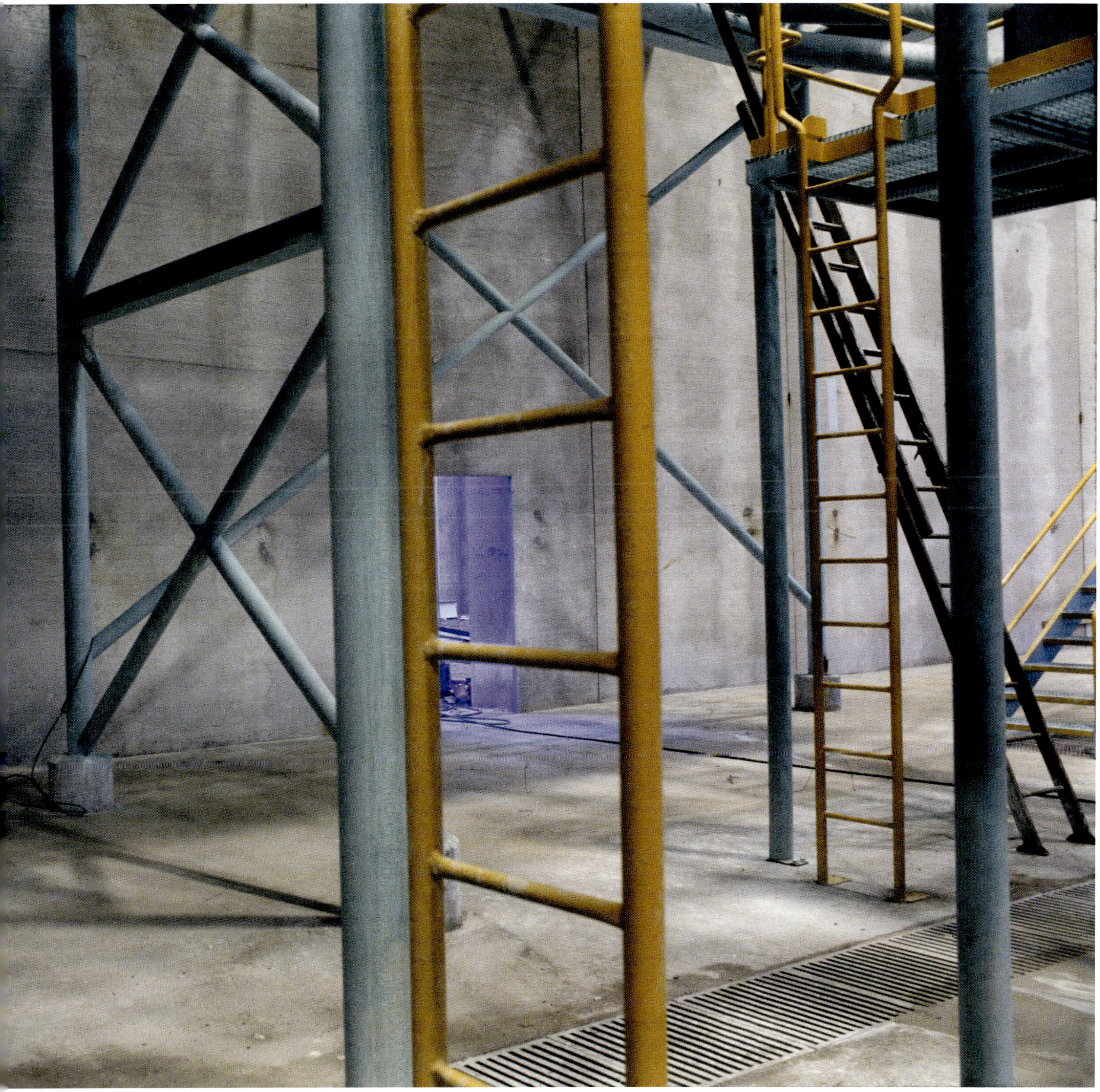

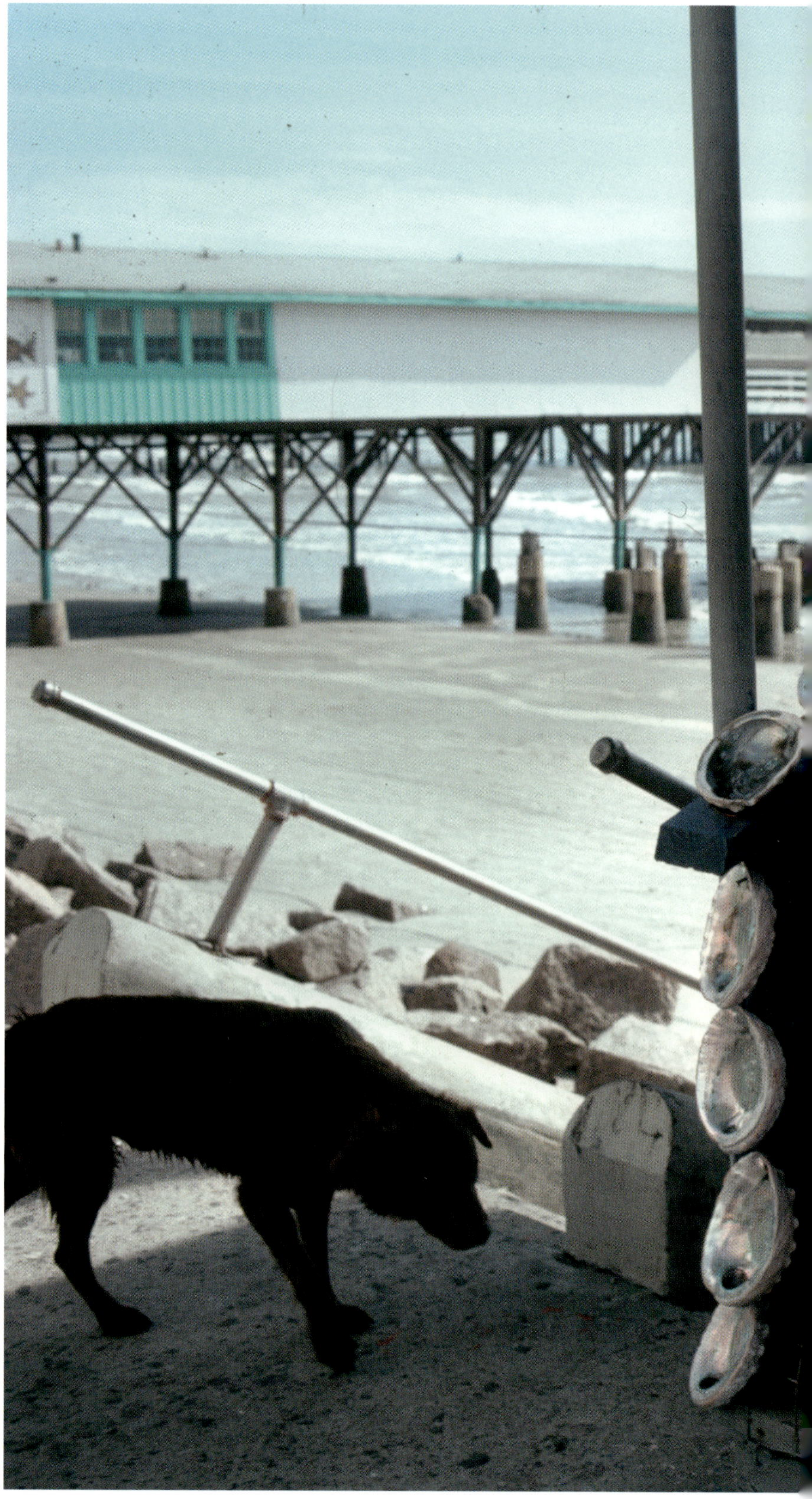

Galveston Beach, Texas, 1981

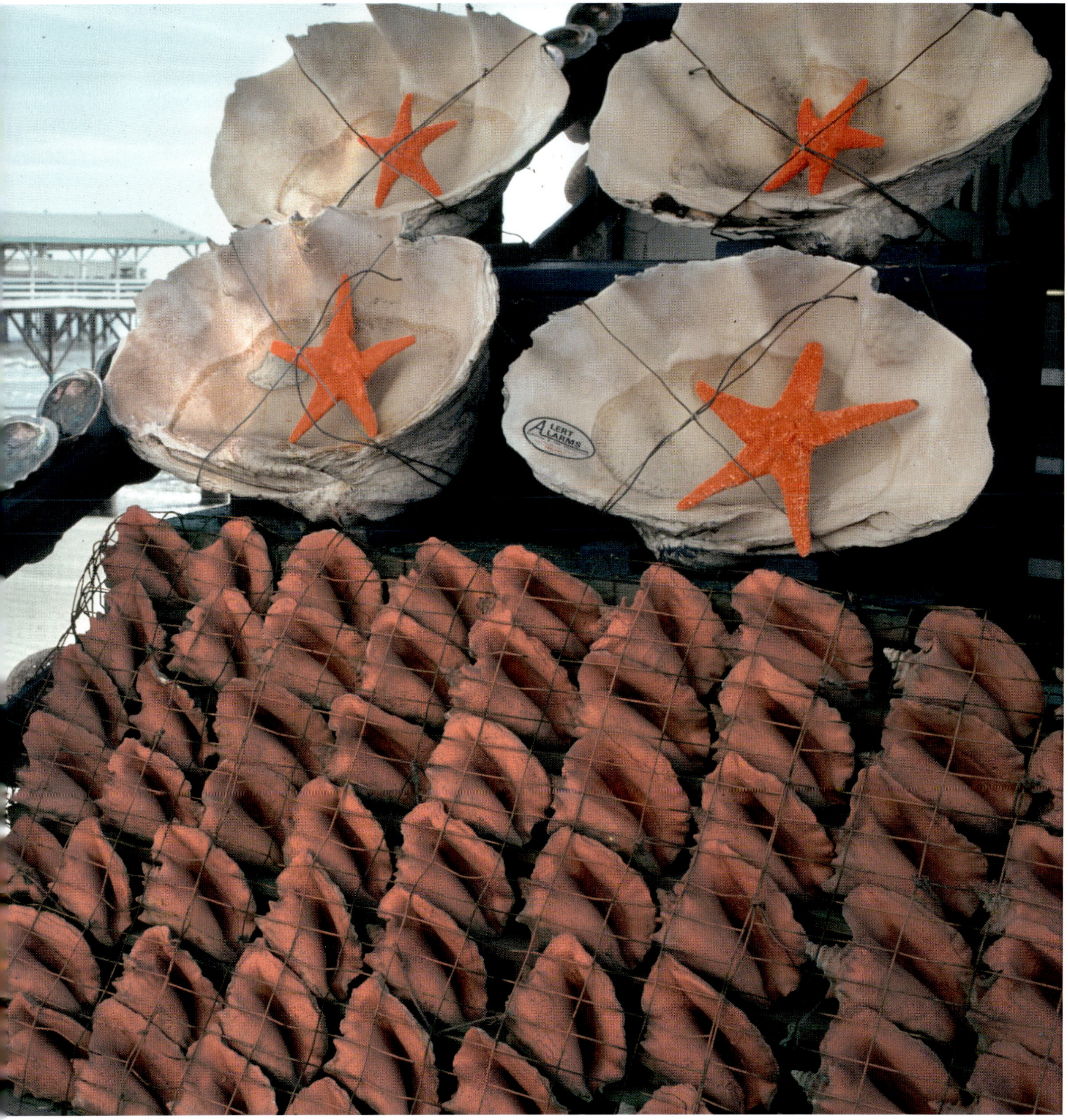
ALERT ALARMS

Buenos Aires, Argentina, 1998

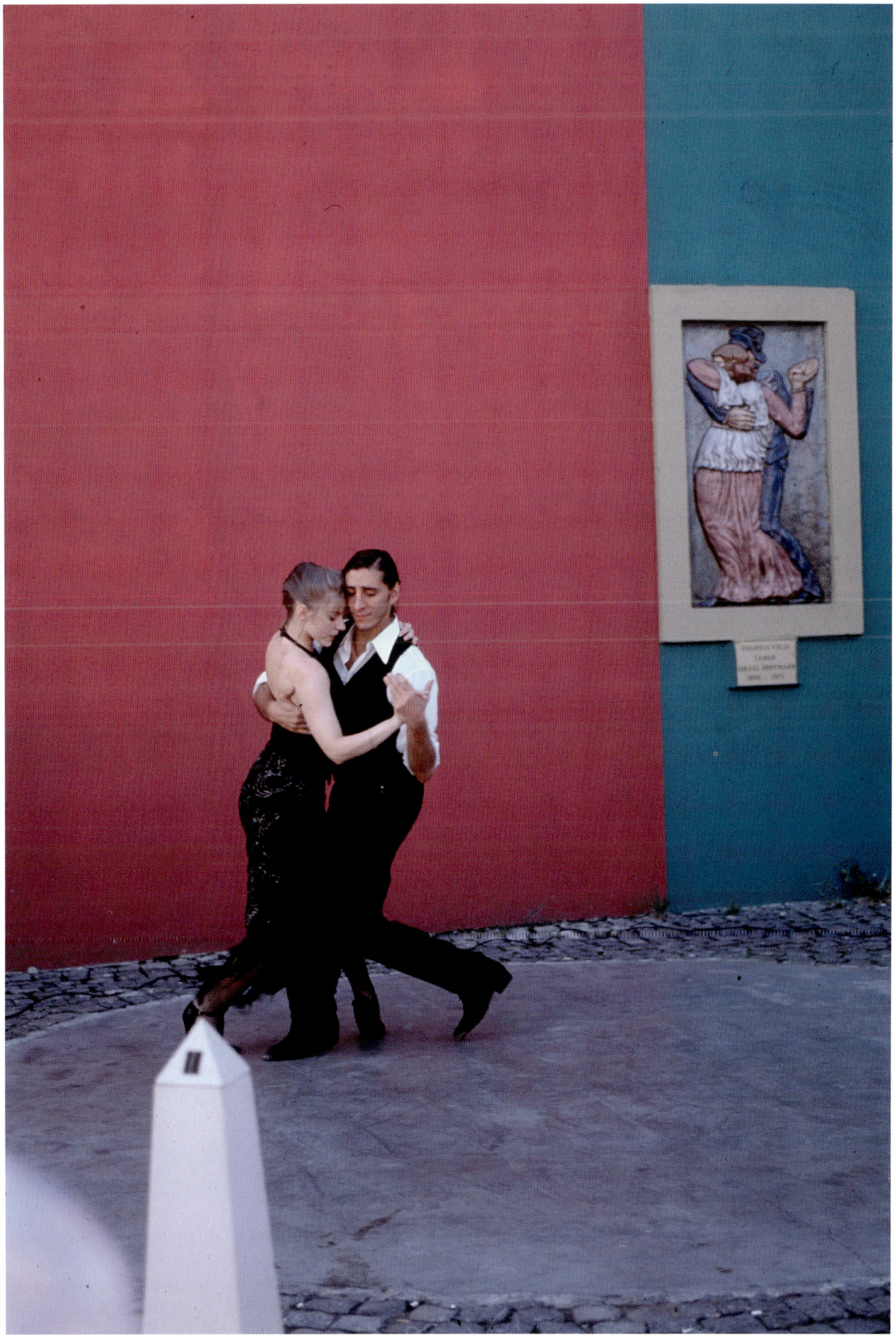

Living Room, Walker Evans House, West Lyme, Connecticut, 1975

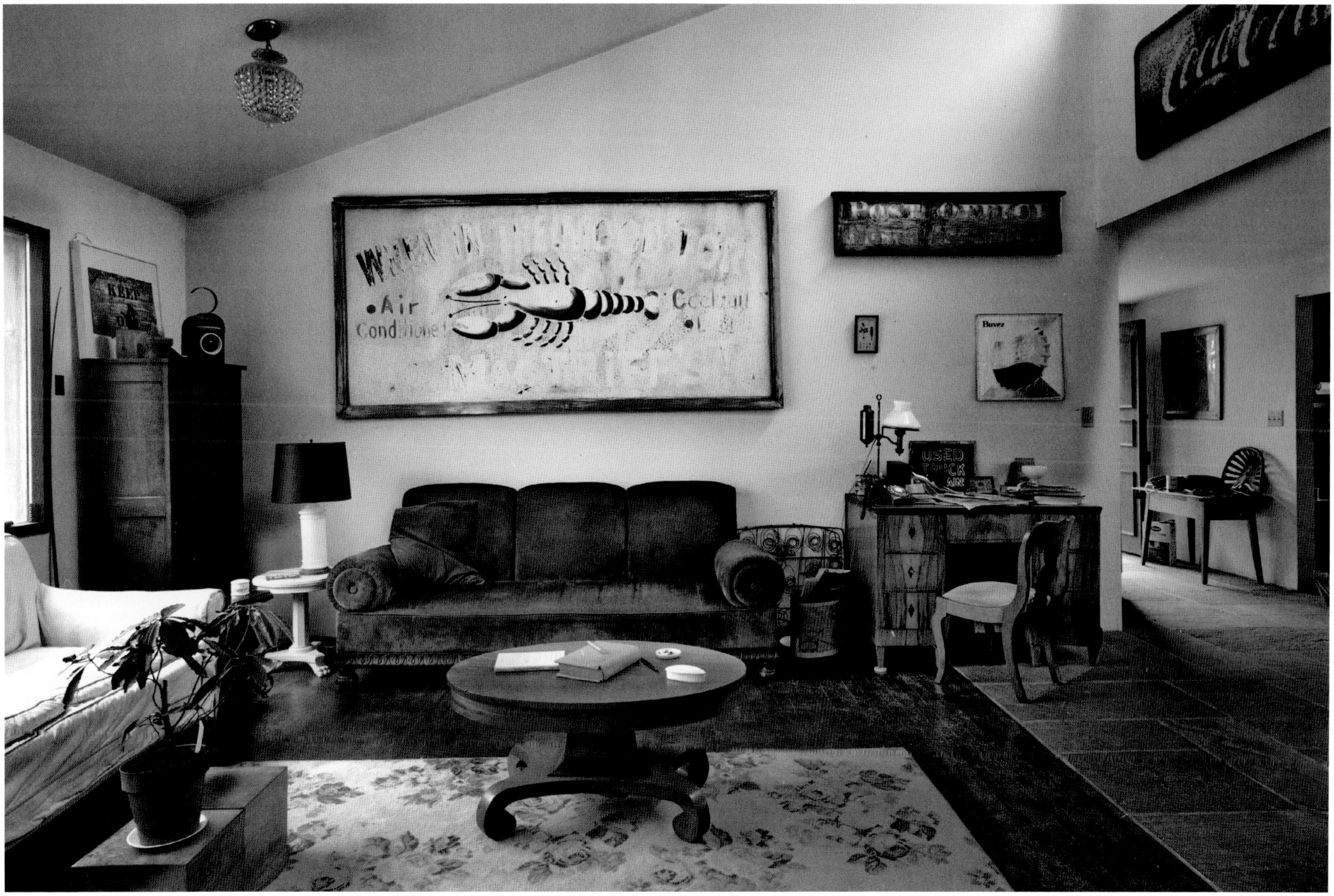
Air
USED
Buvez

74

Bathroom, Walker Evans House, West Lyme, Connecticut, 1975

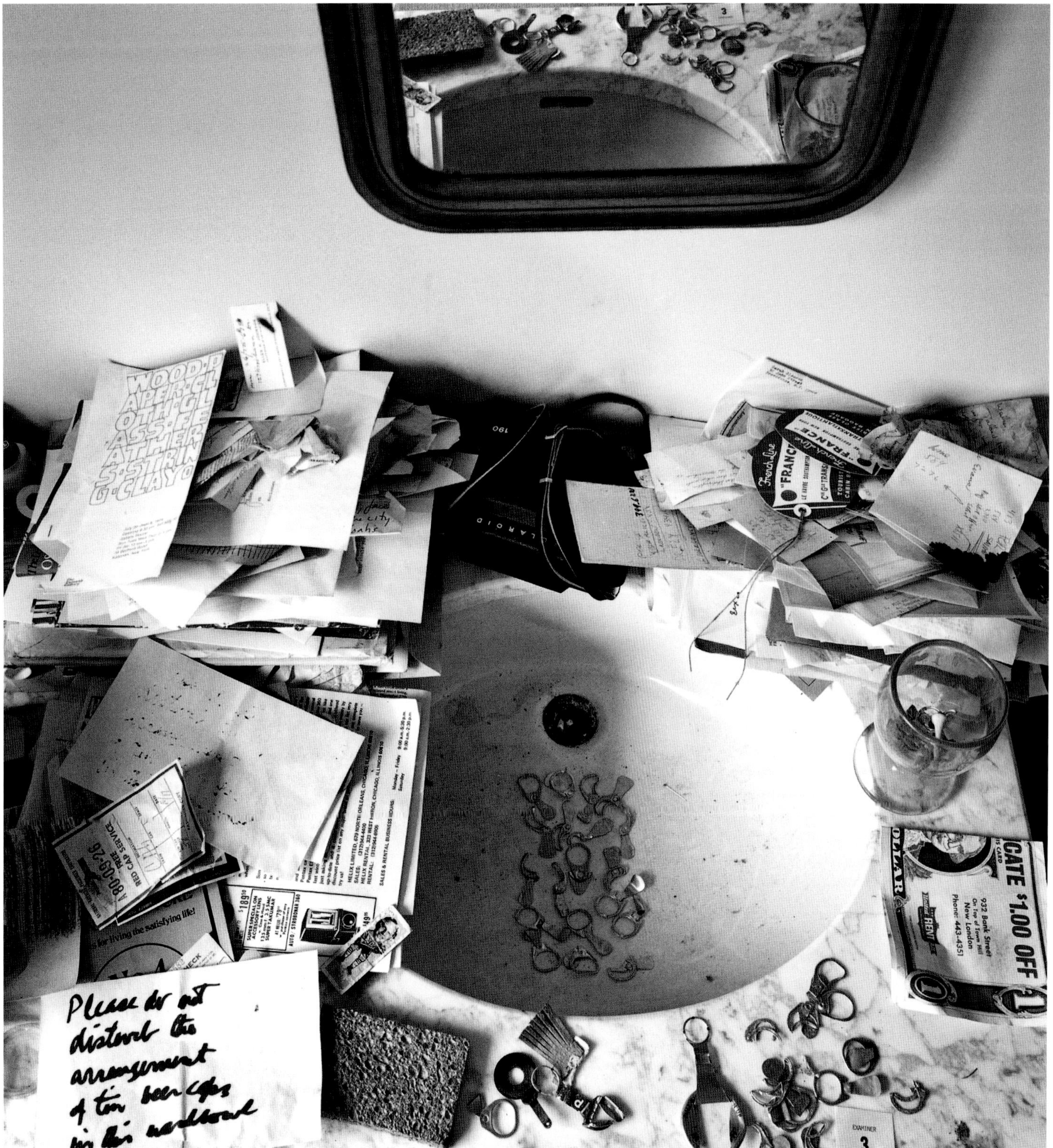
$1.00 OFF
EXAMINER
3
RED CAP SERVICE

A grouping of Evans's collected objects reflecting his original arrangement of April, 1975

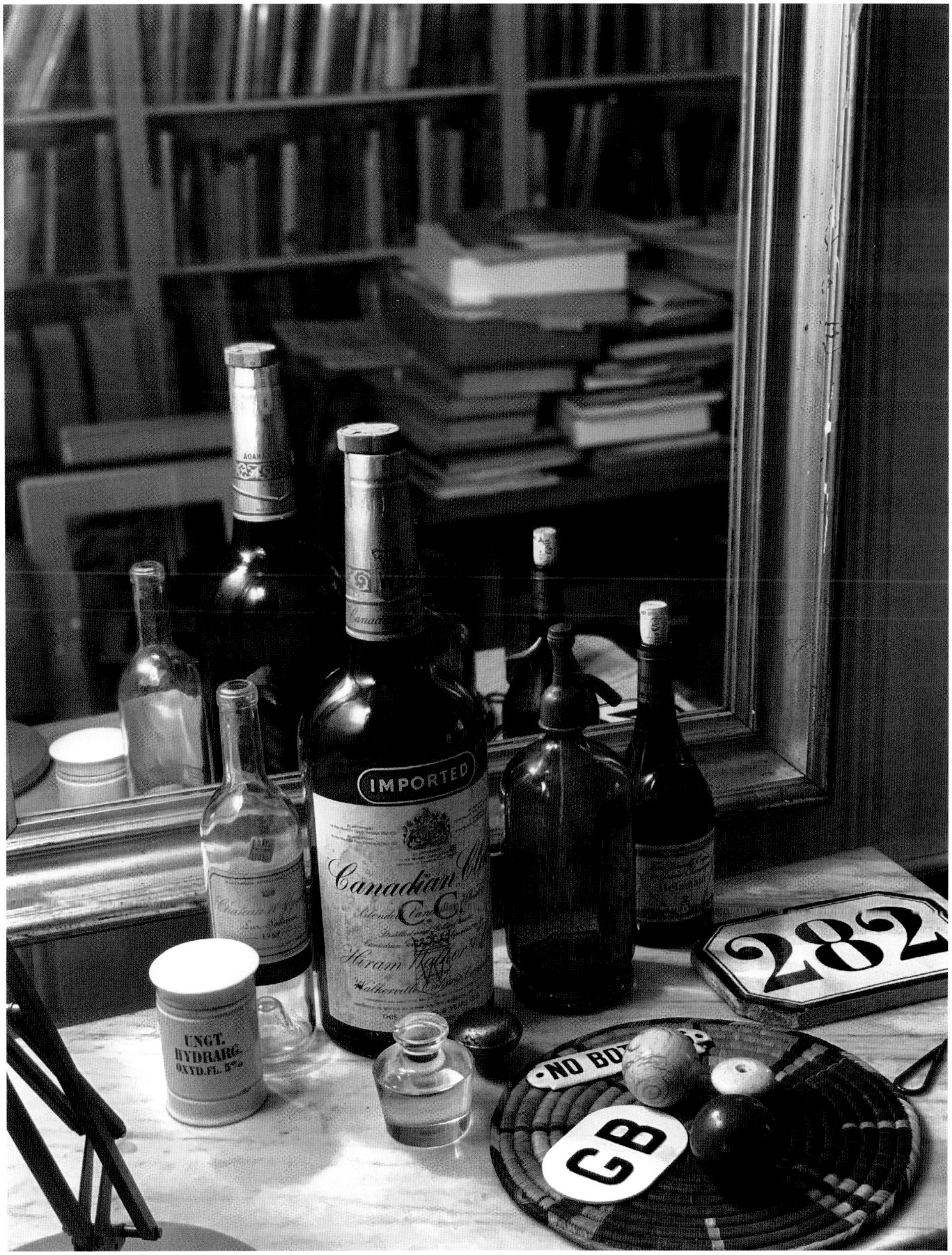
IMPORTED
UNGT.
HYDRARG.
282
GB

78

Edna Lewis, Duane Park at Hudson Street, New York, 1983

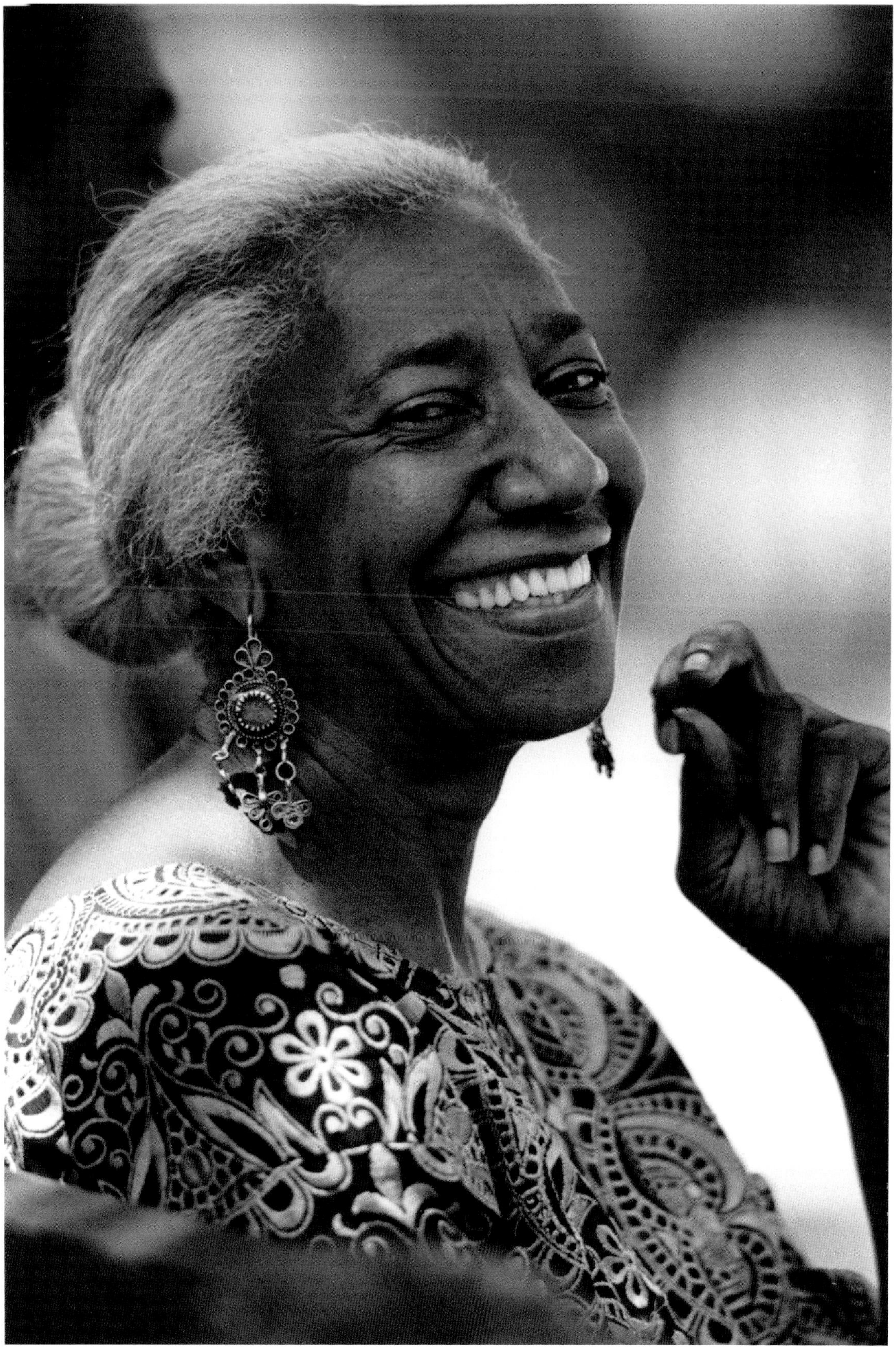

80

Edna Lewis and her niece Nina Williams
Orange County, Virginia, June, 1971

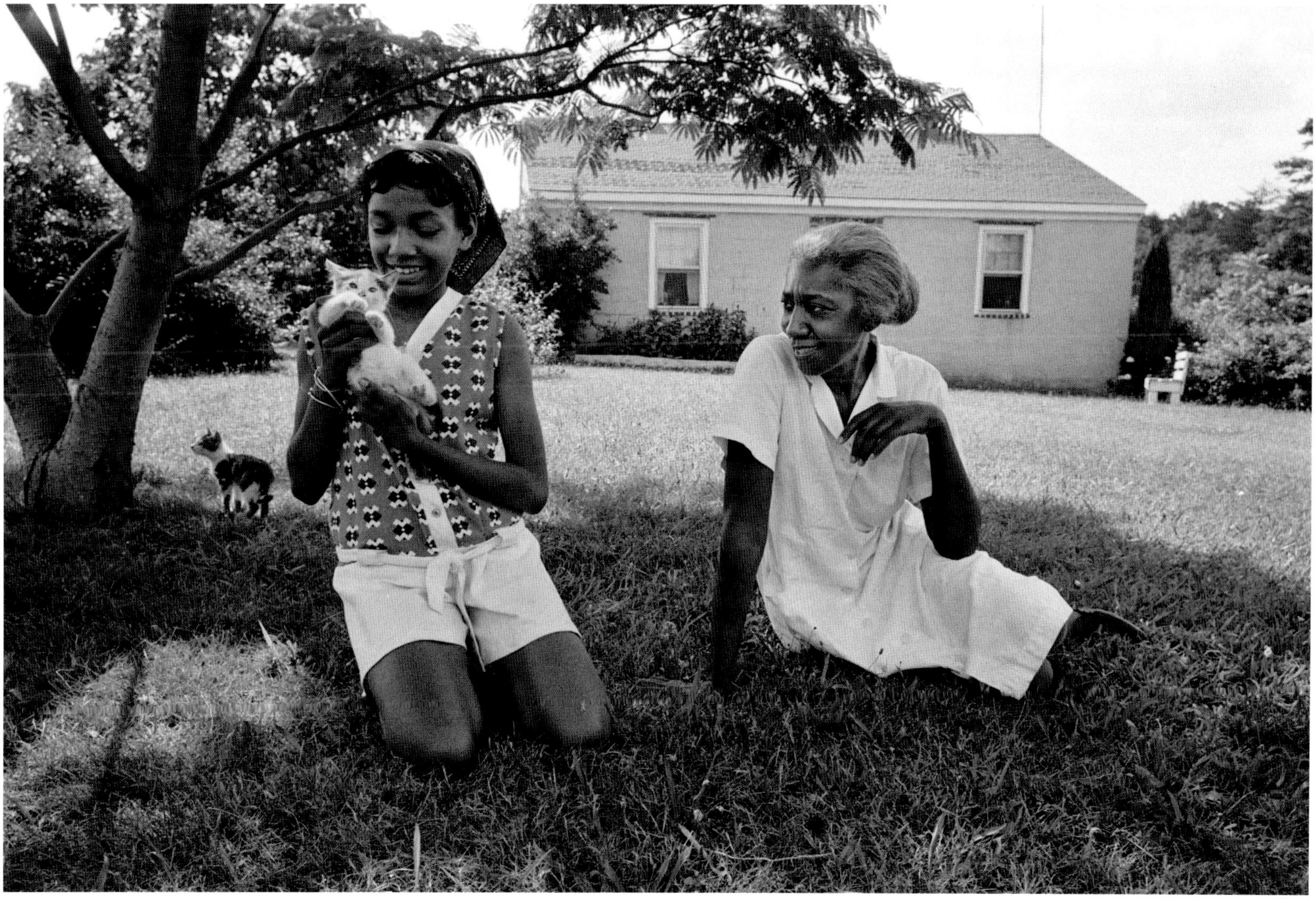

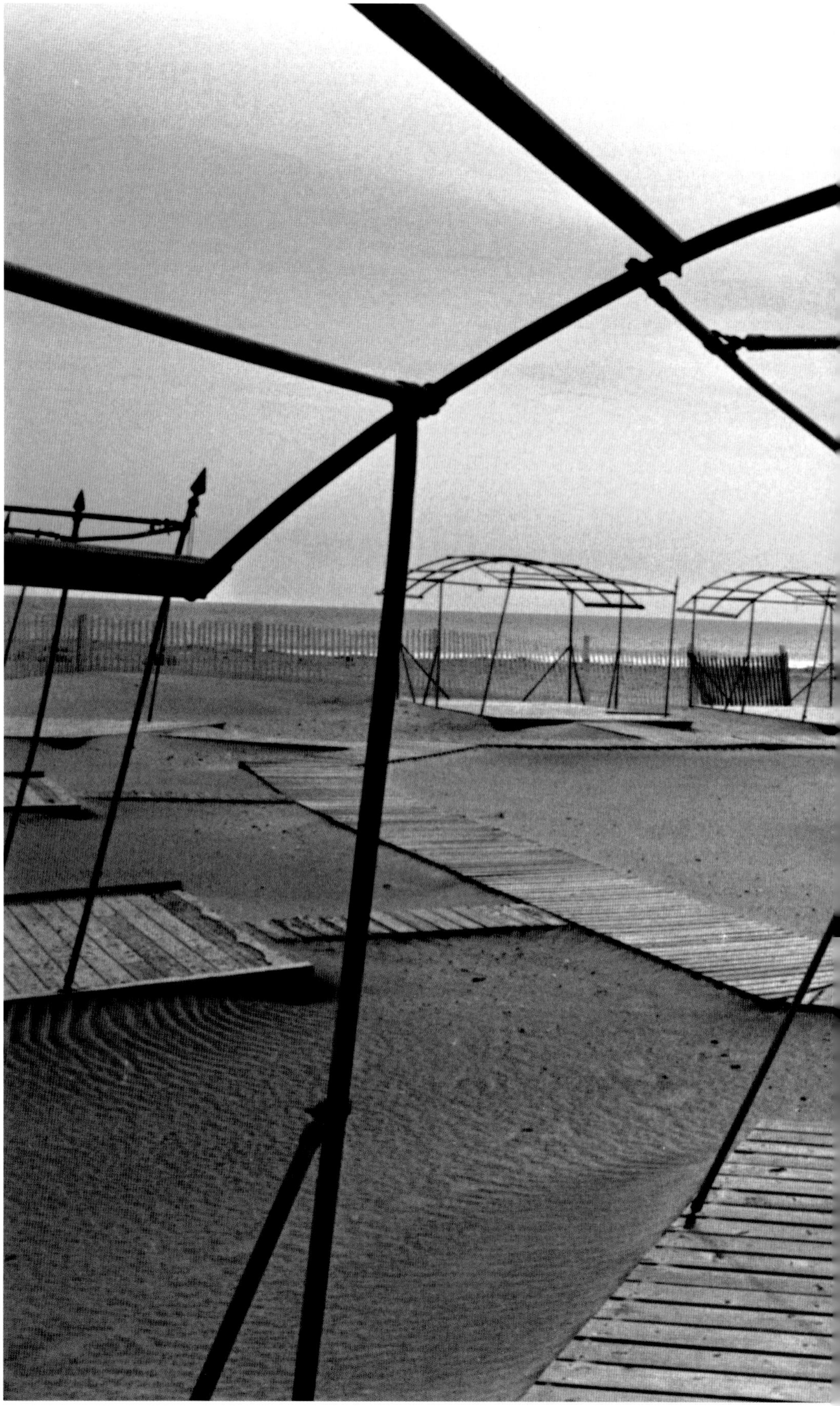

Atlantic City, New Jersey, 1975

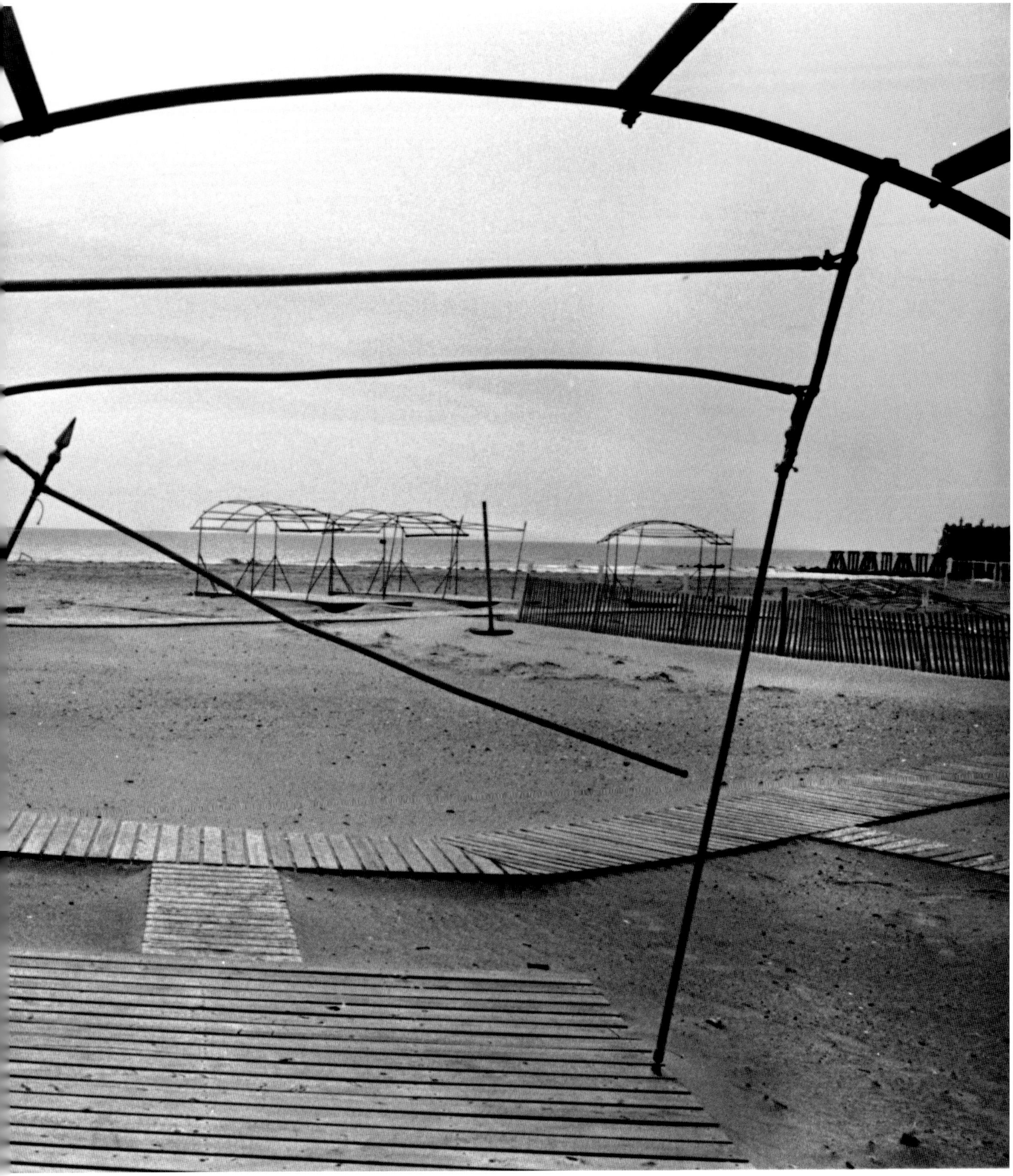

84

Bronx, New York, n.d.

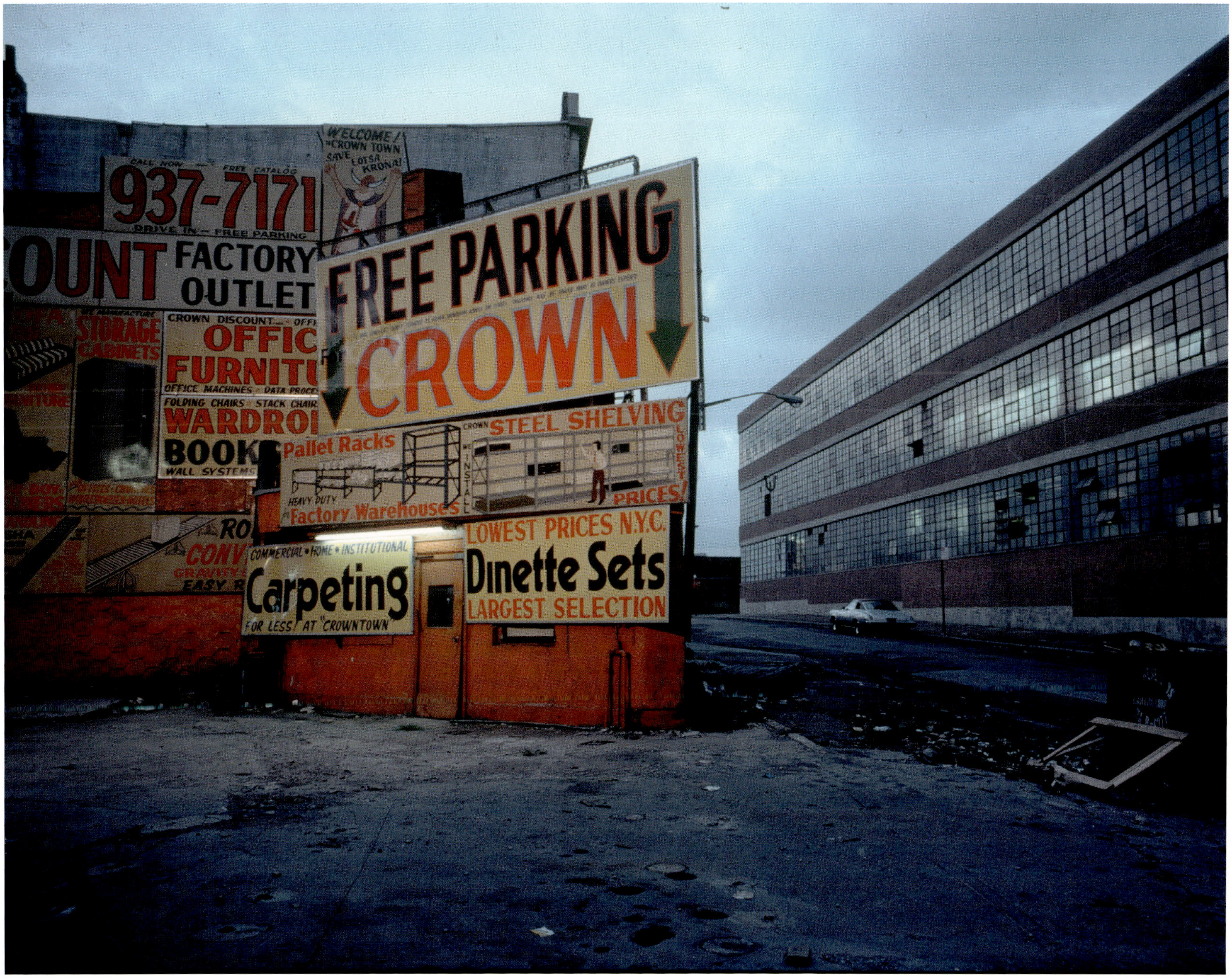
WELCOME!
"CROWN TOWN"
SAVE LOTSA KRONA!
CALL NOW — FREE CATALOG
937-7171
DRIVE IN — FREE PARKING
FACTORY OUTLET
STORAGE CABINETS
CROWN DISCOUNT
WAREHOUSE
BOOK
WALL SYSTEMS
FREE PARKING
CROWN
Pallet Racks
CROWN STEEL SHELVING
HEAVY DUTY
Factory Warehouses
INSTALL
LOWEST PRICES!
LOWEST PRICES N.Y.C.
Dinette Sets
LARGEST SELECTION
COMMERCIAL • HOME • INSTITUTIONAL
Carpeting
FOR LESS! AT "CROWNTOWN"

West Side Highway in the 40s, New York, ca. 1984

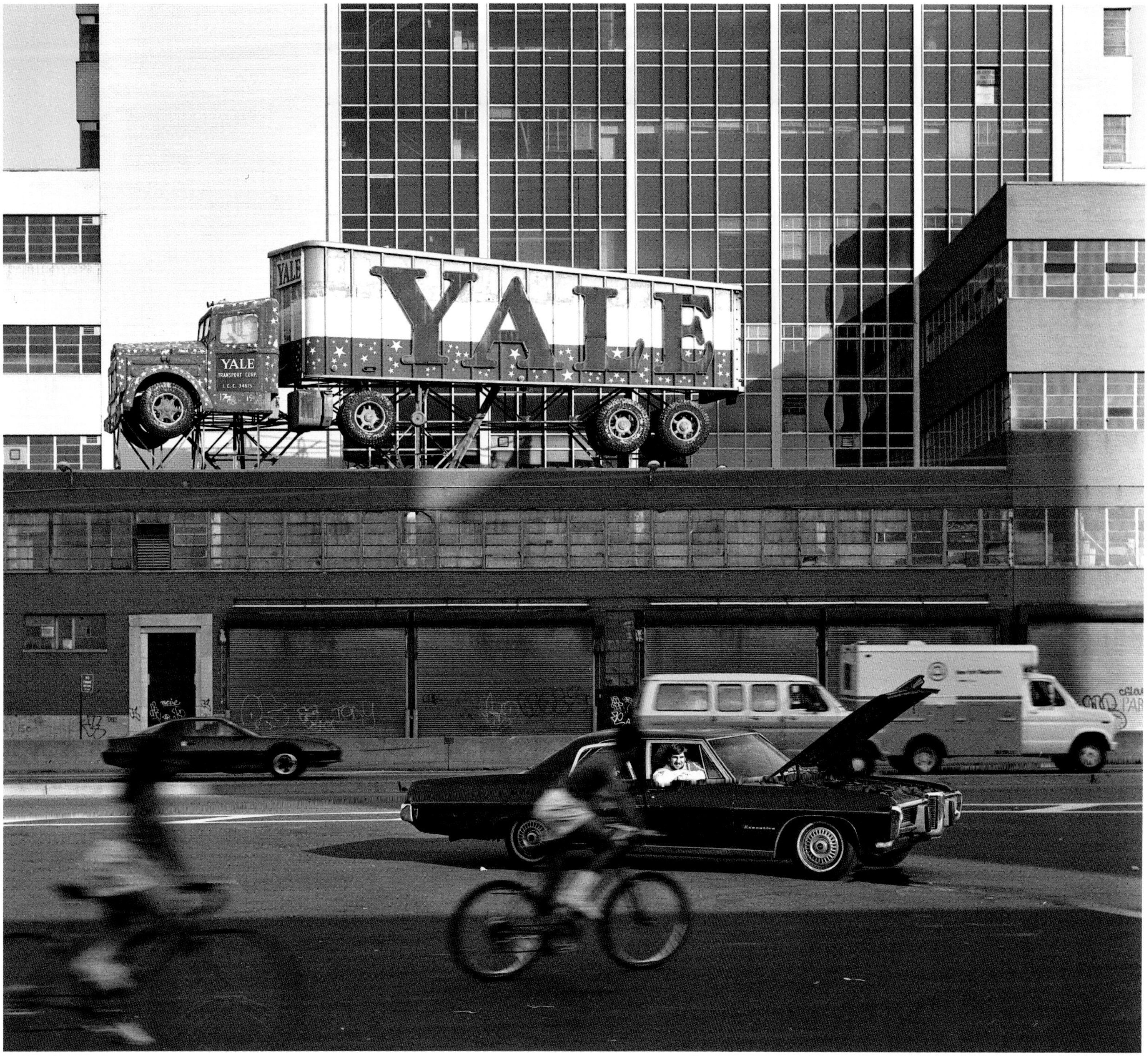
YALE
YALE
TRANSPORT CORP.
I.C.C. 34815
YALE

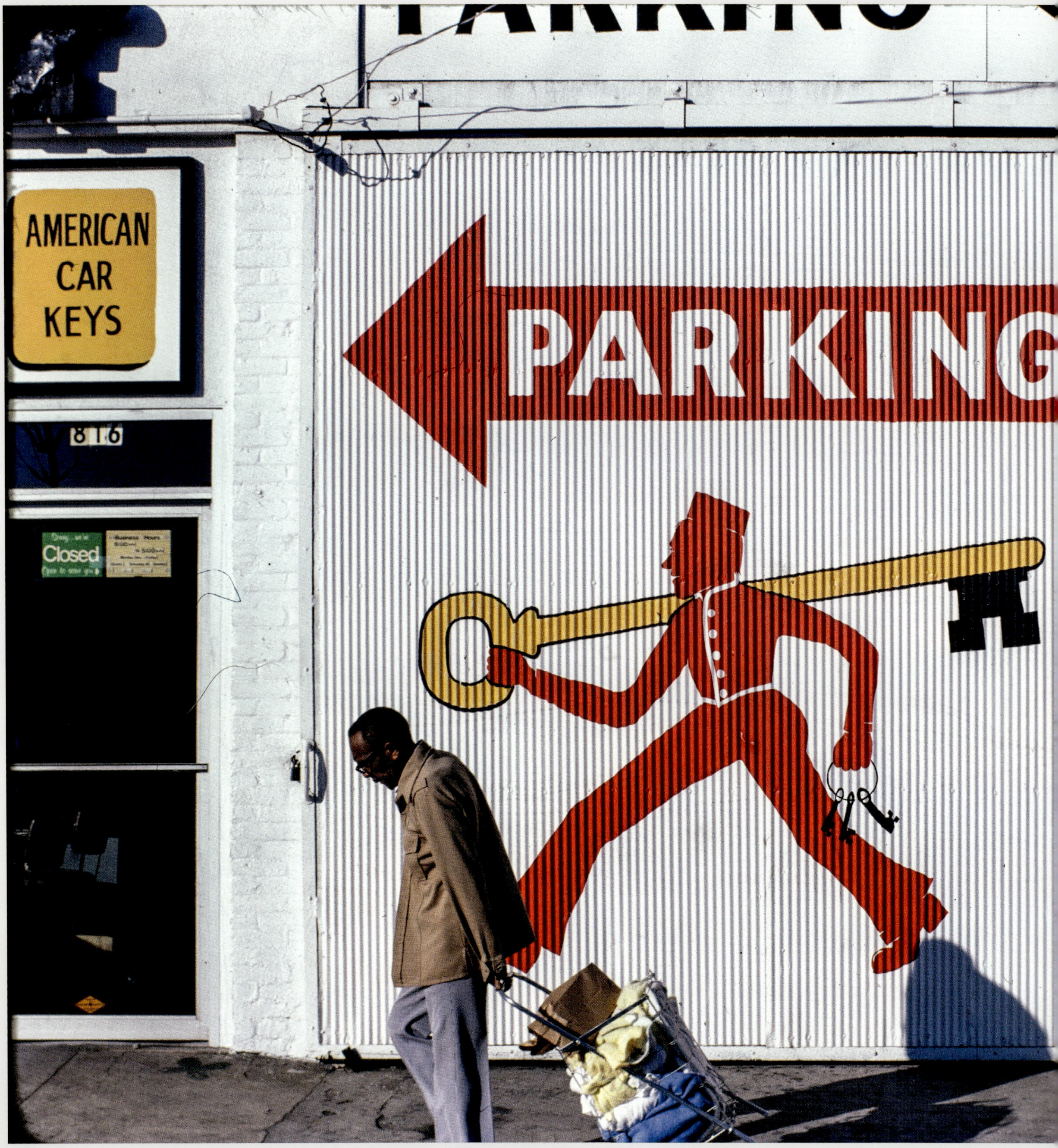
AMERICAN
CAR
KEYS
816
Closed
PARKING

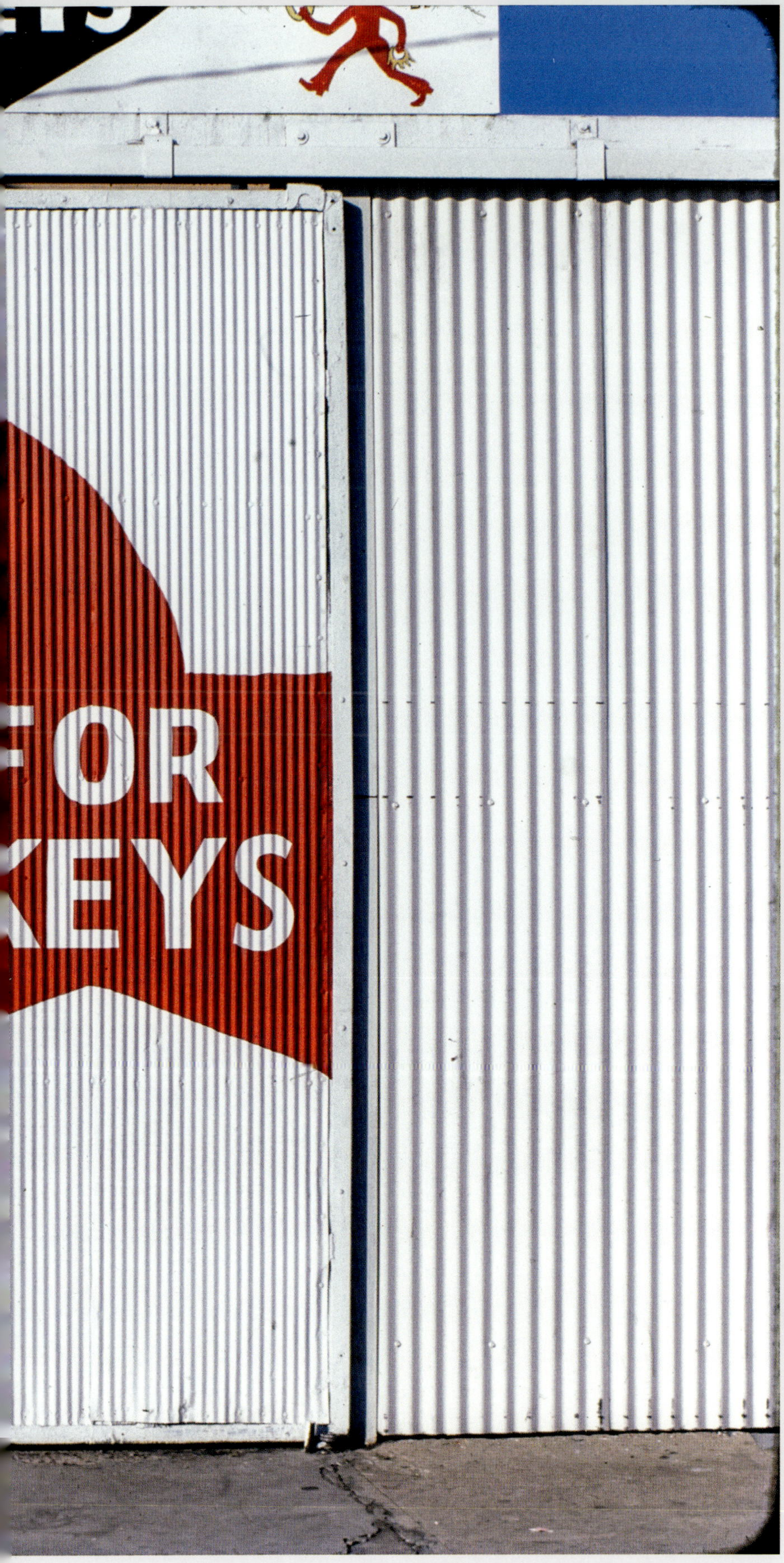

Untitled, California, n.d.

90

Hall County, Georgia, 2008

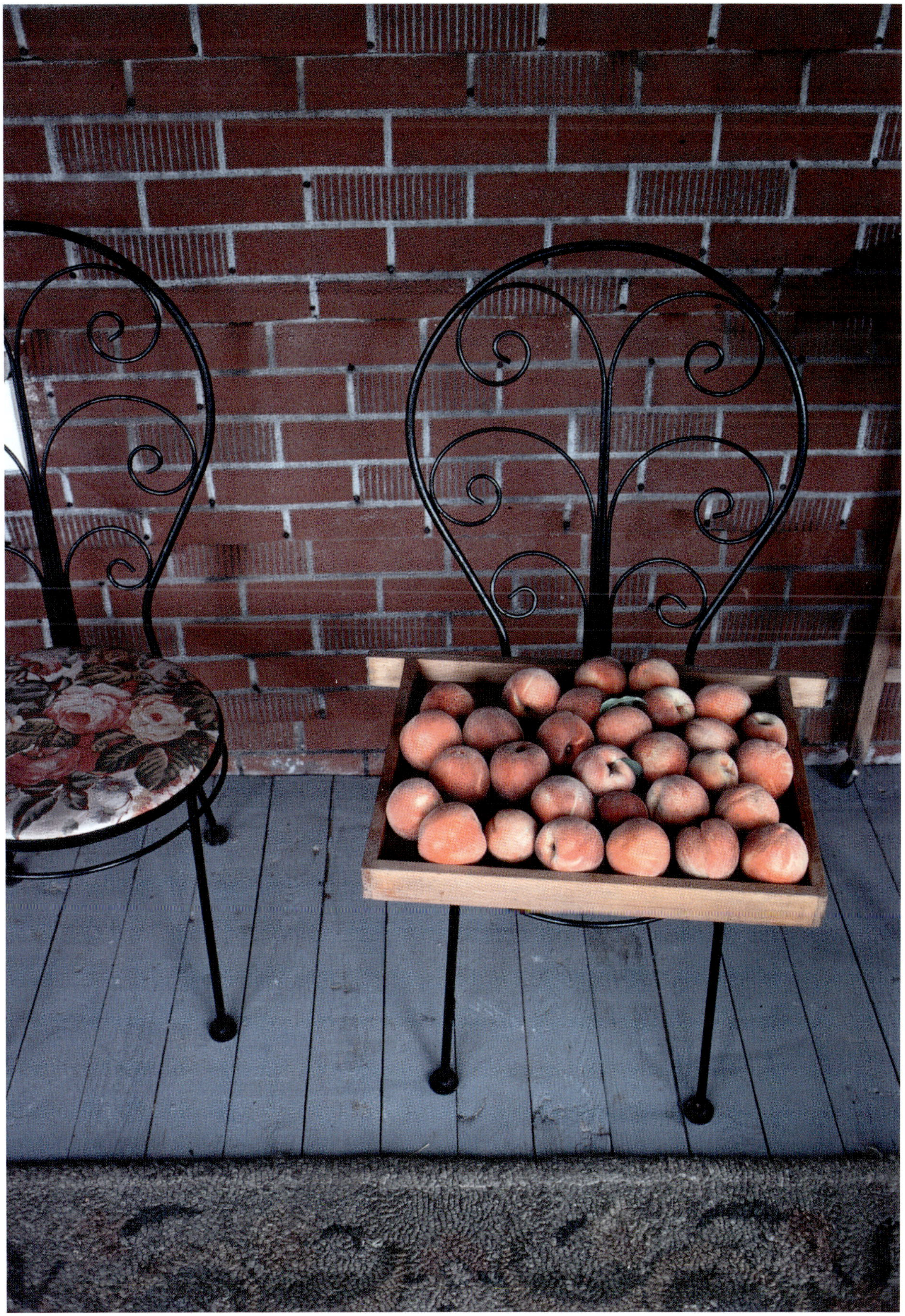

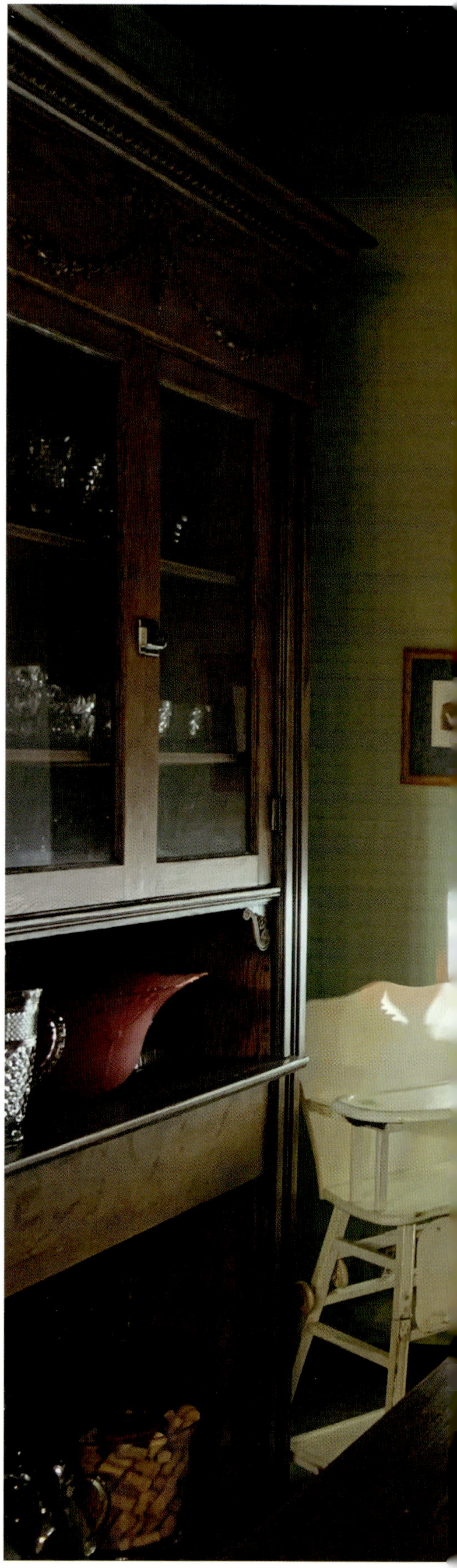

Jarrett House, Hall County, Georgia, 2017

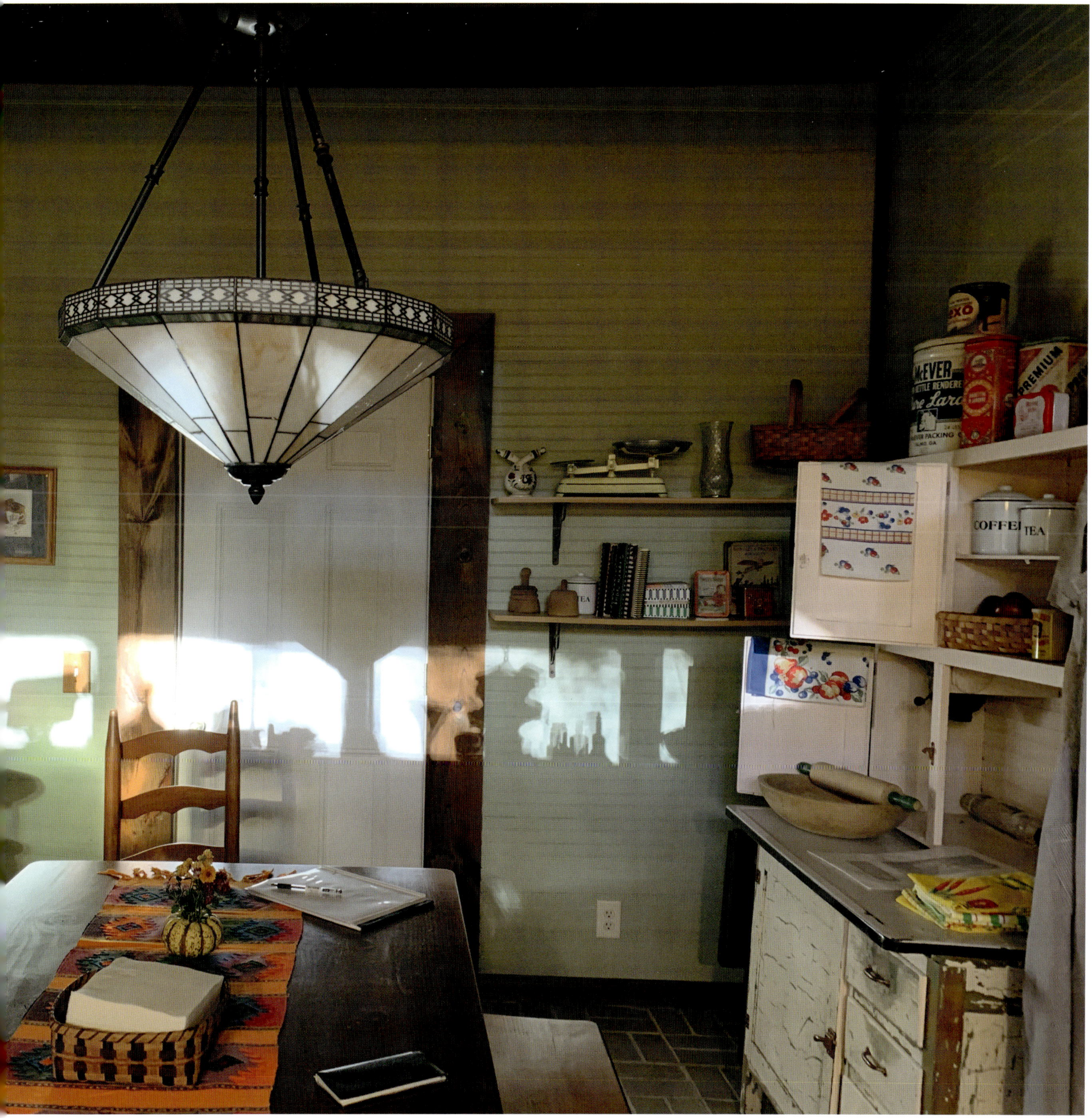
McEVER
PREMIUM
TEA

Unity Church Graveyard, Jackson County, Georgia, 2008

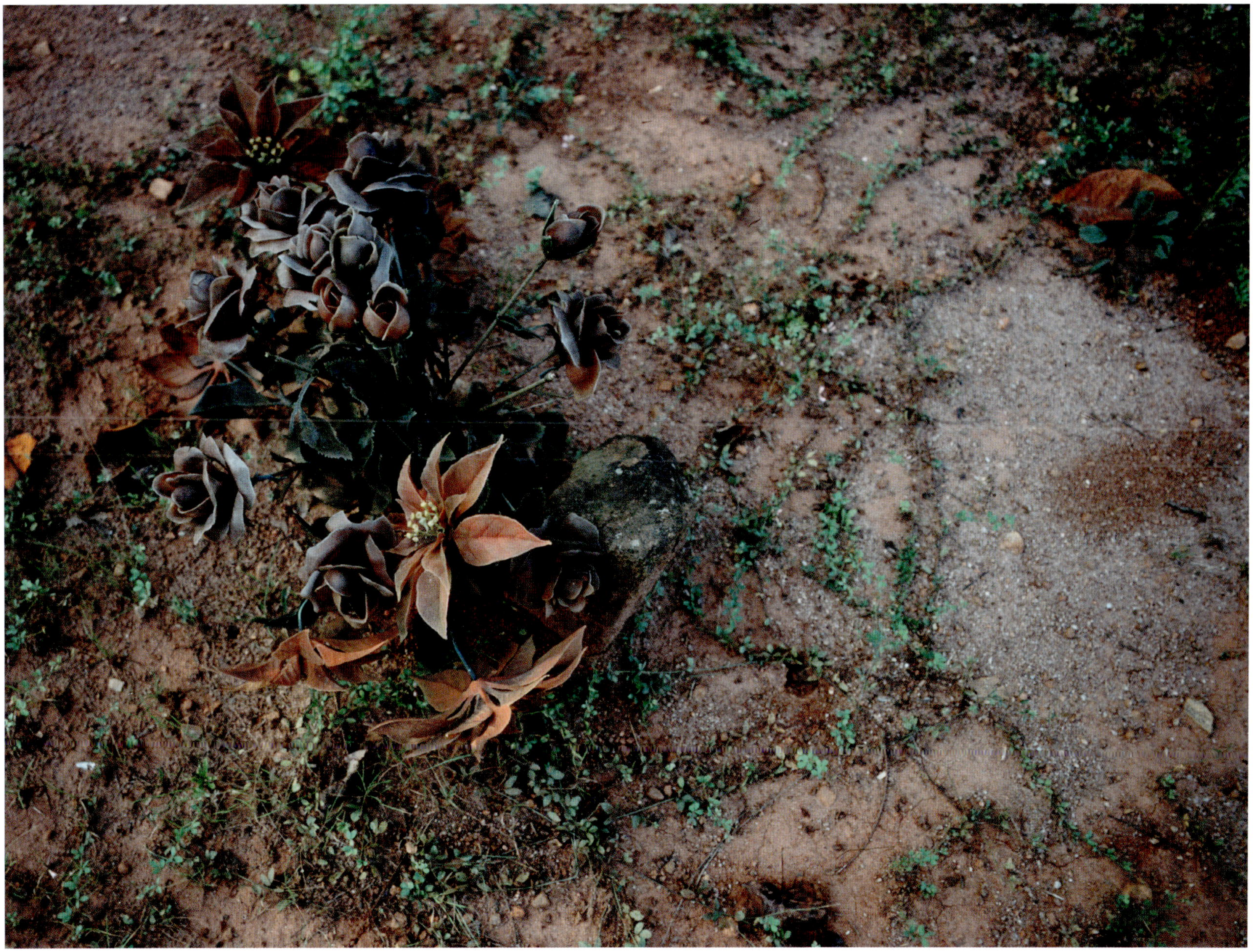

Untitled, Still Life, ca. 1990

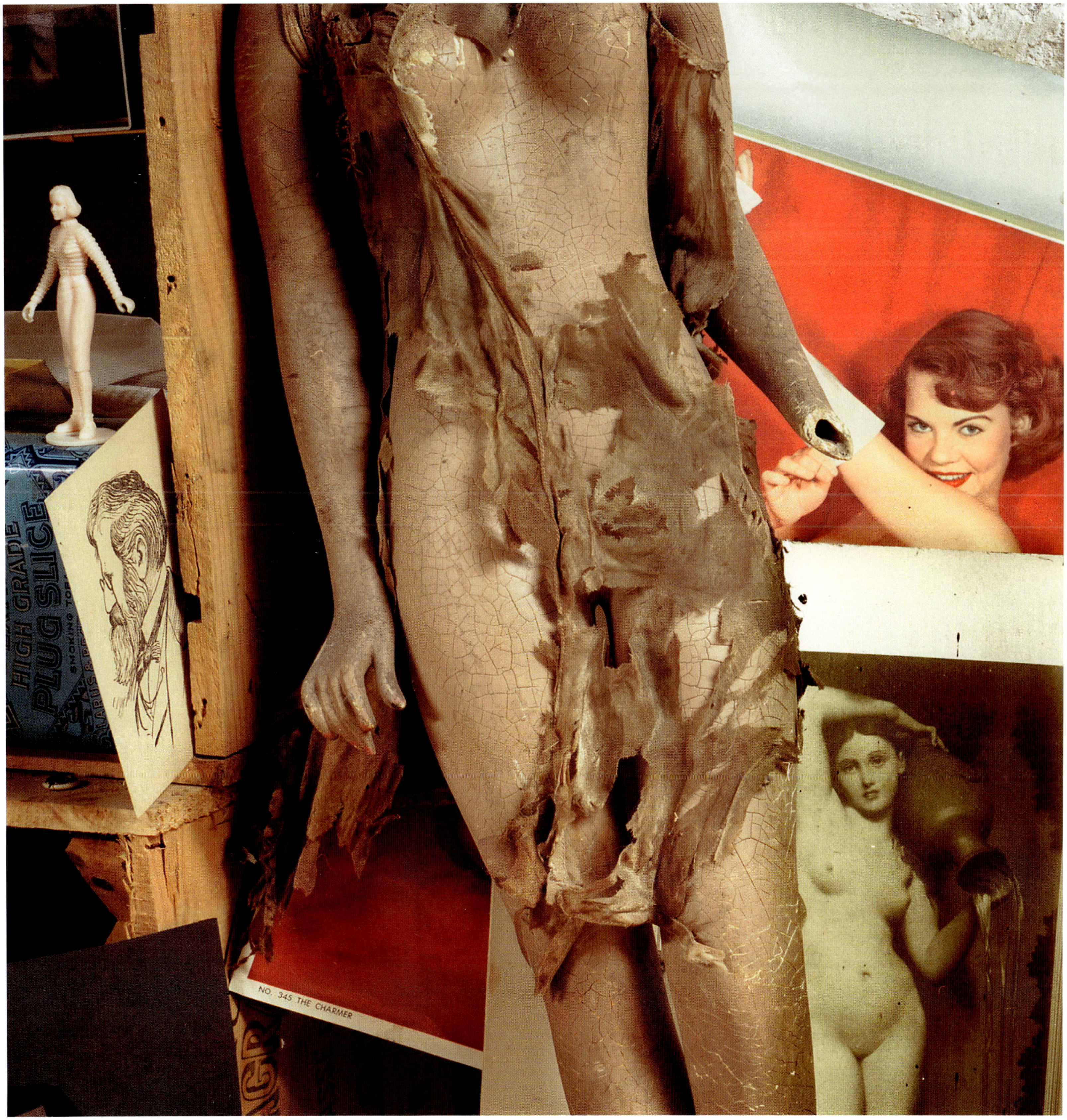
HIGH GRADE
PLUG SLICE
NO. 345 THE CHARMER

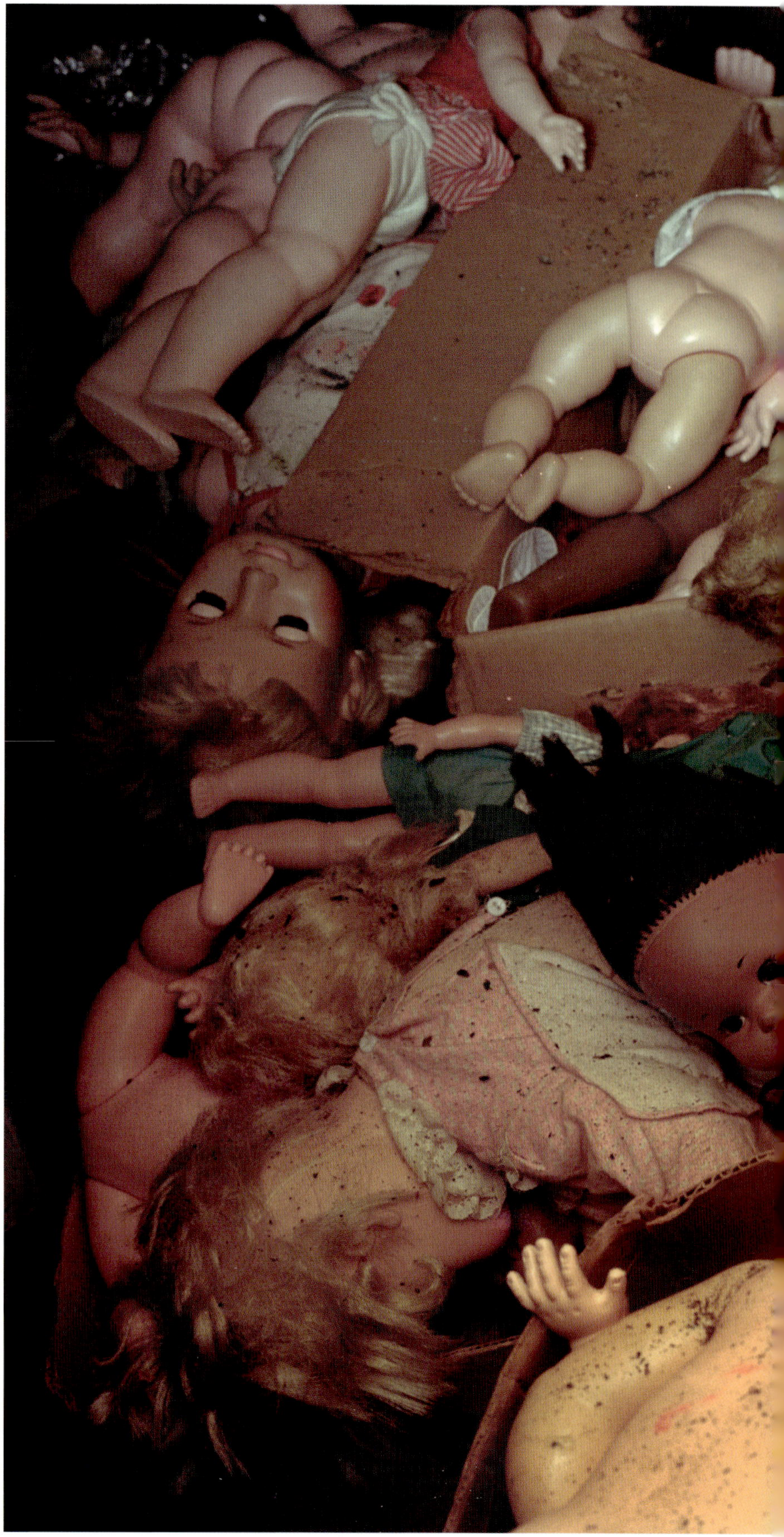

Attic, Marietta, Georgia, 2007

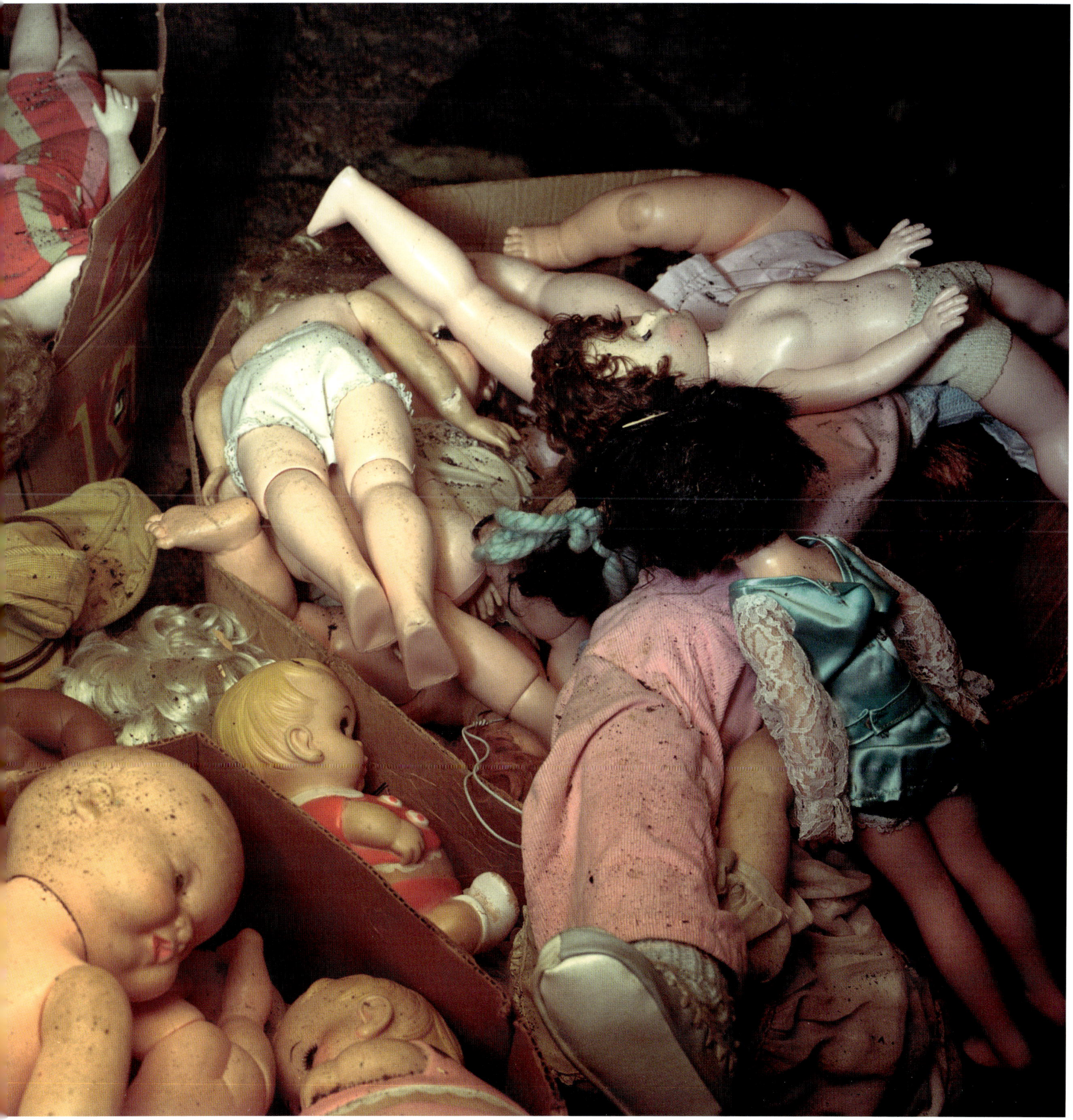

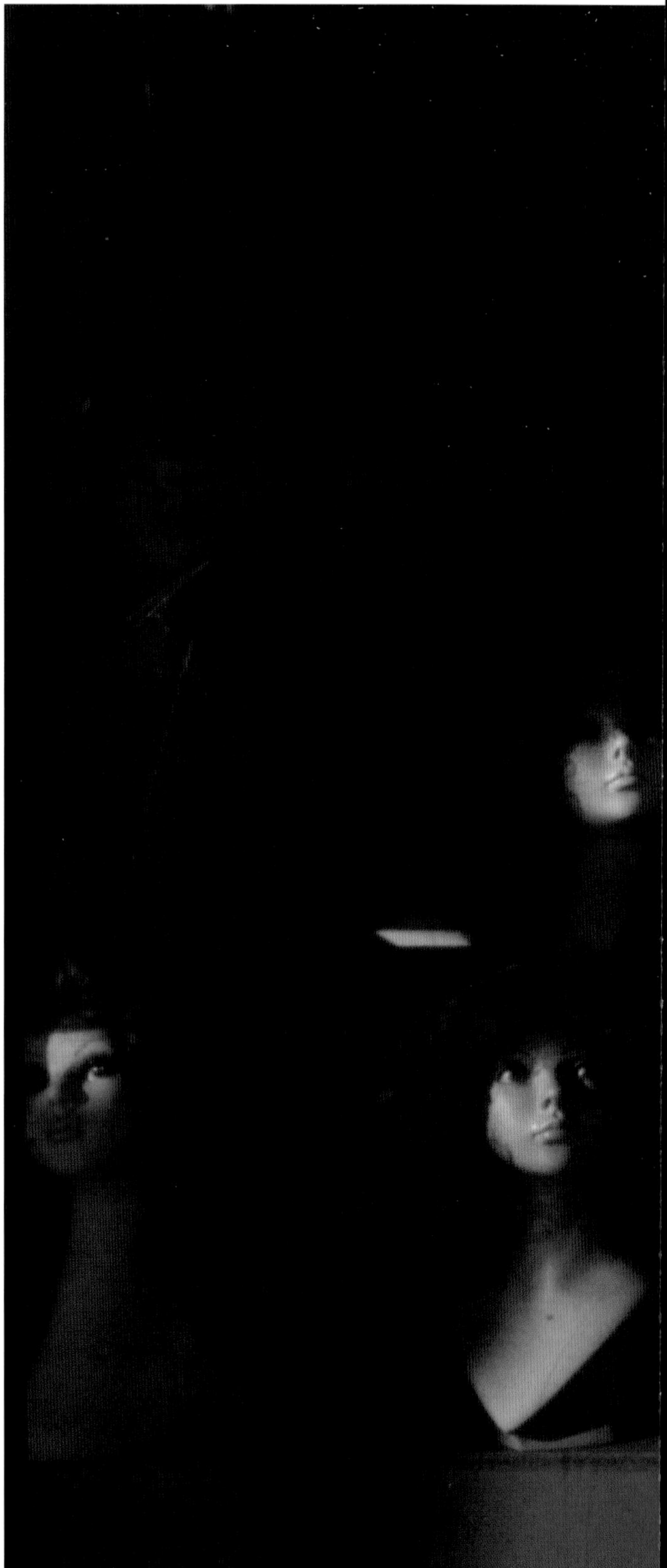

Lower Chapel Street, New Haven, 1981

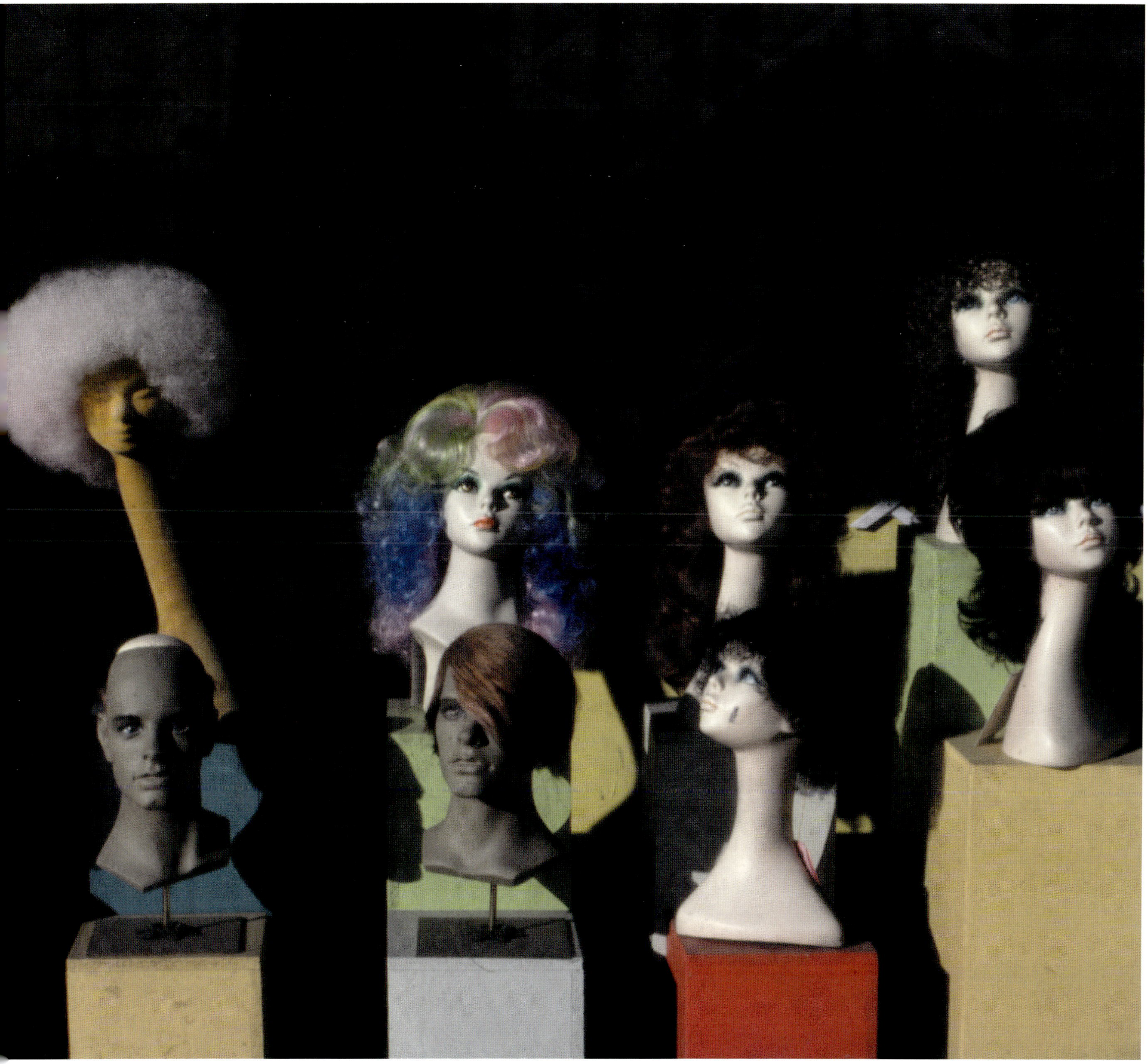

Trafalgar Square, London, ca. 1975

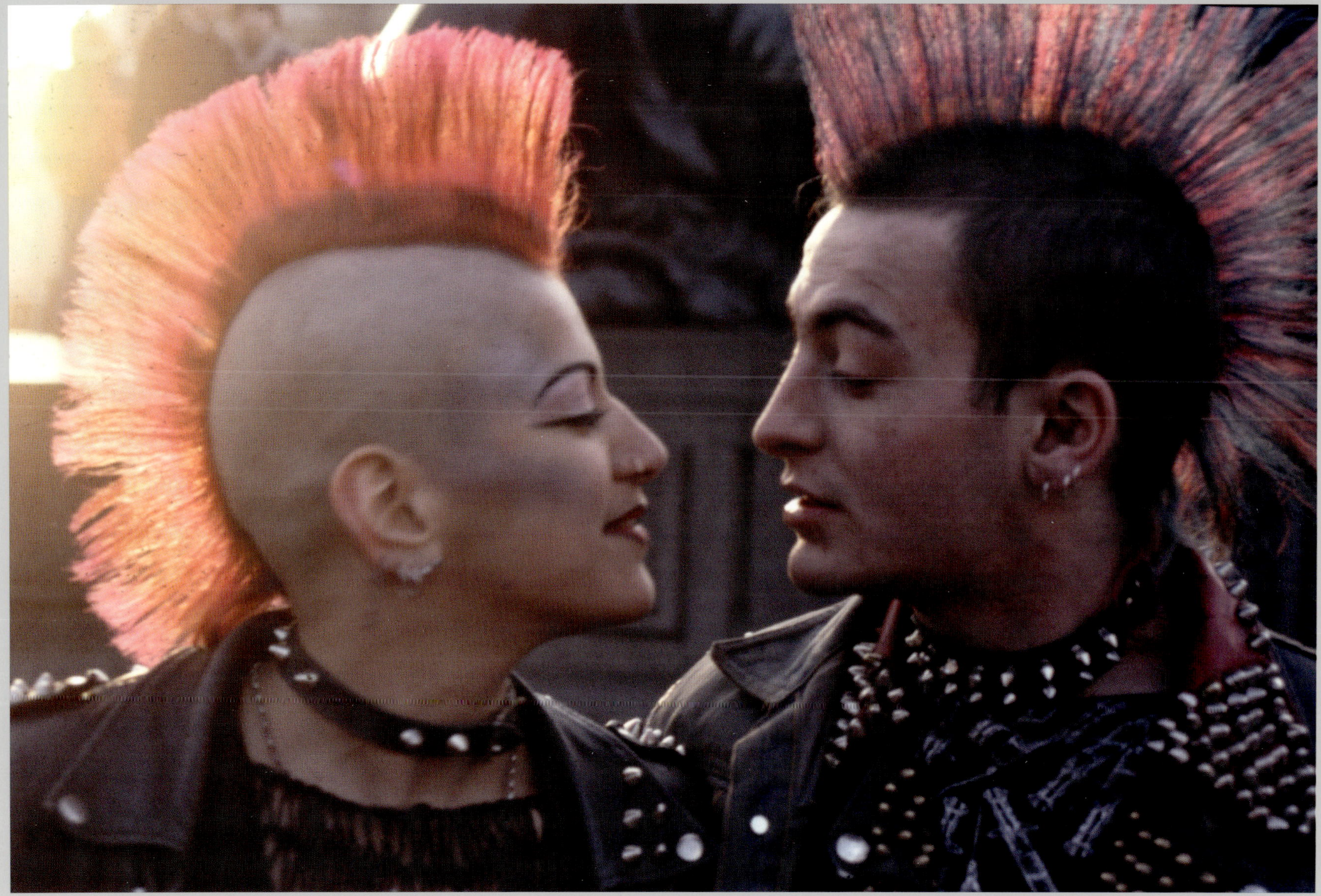

Graffiti, Duane Park near Hudson Street, New York, 1982

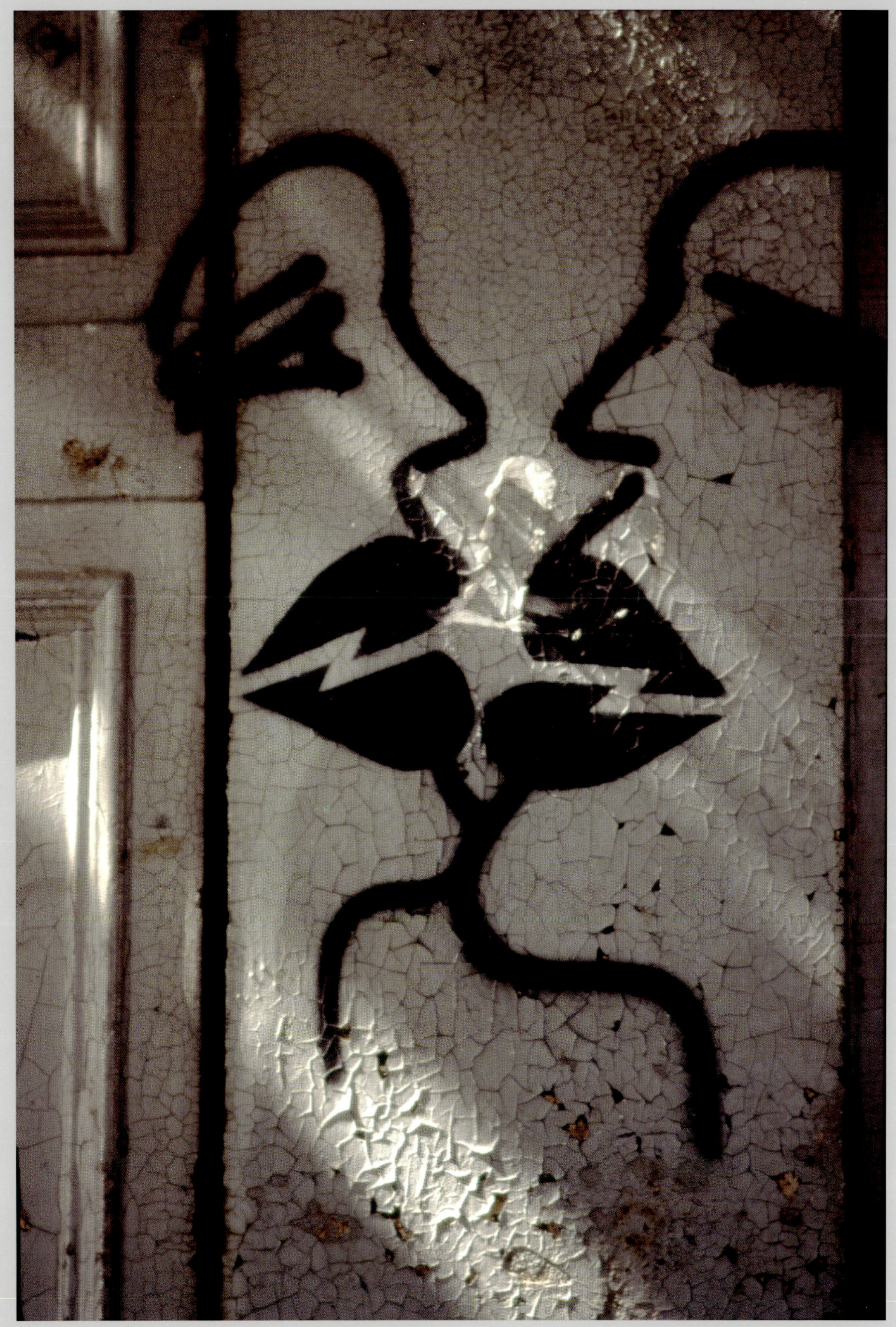

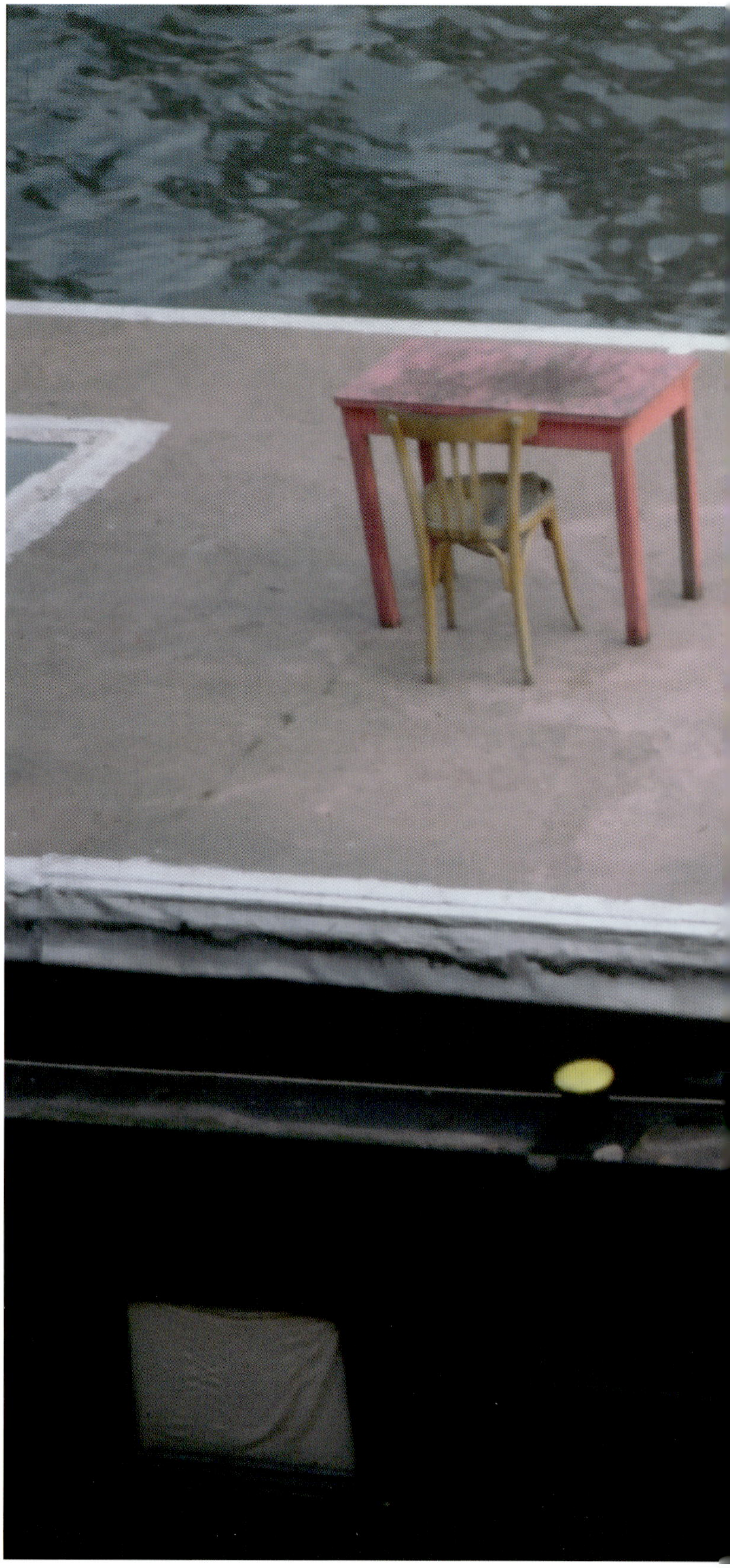

Houseboat, Thames River, London

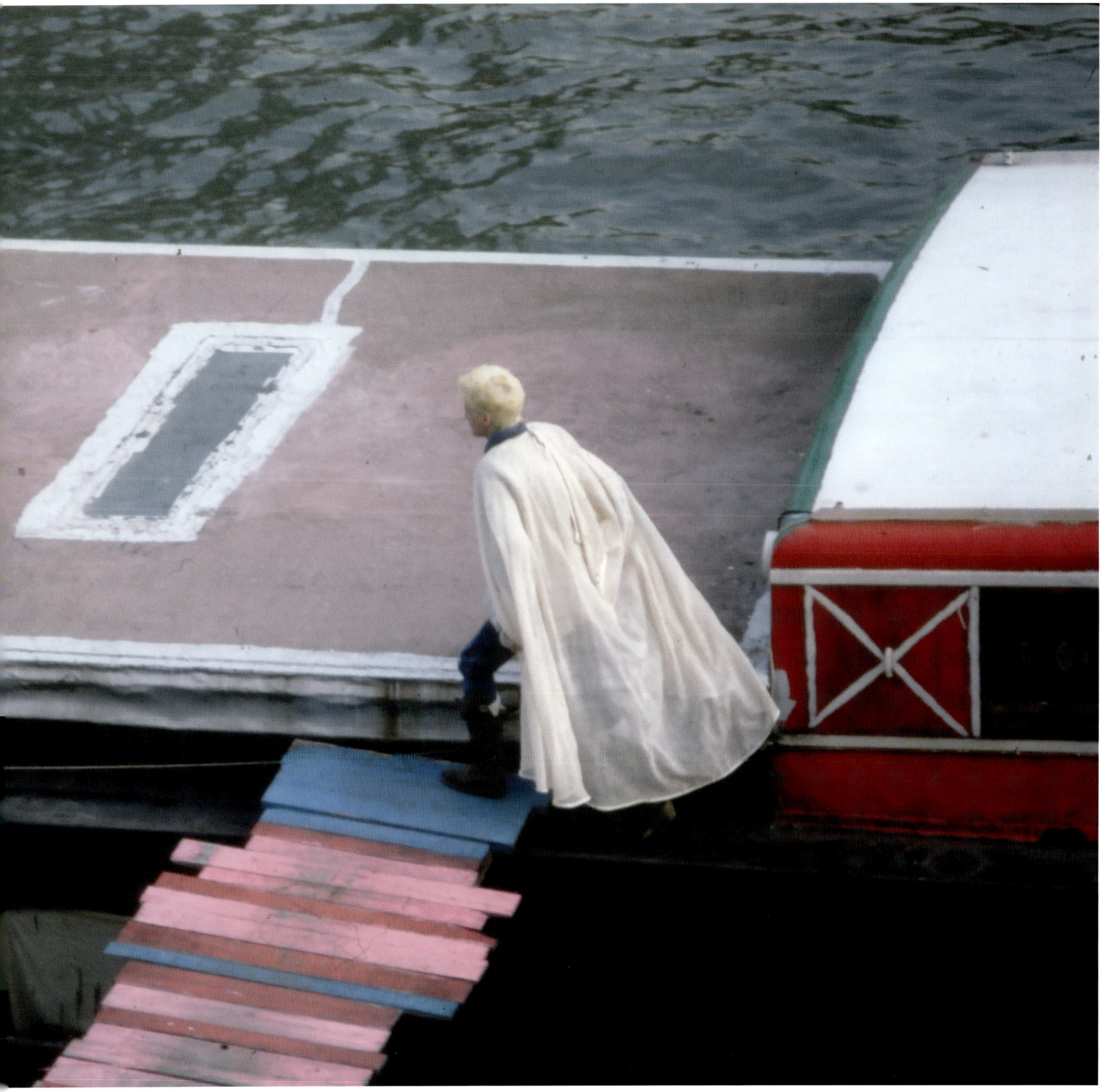

108

Bronx, New York, n.d.

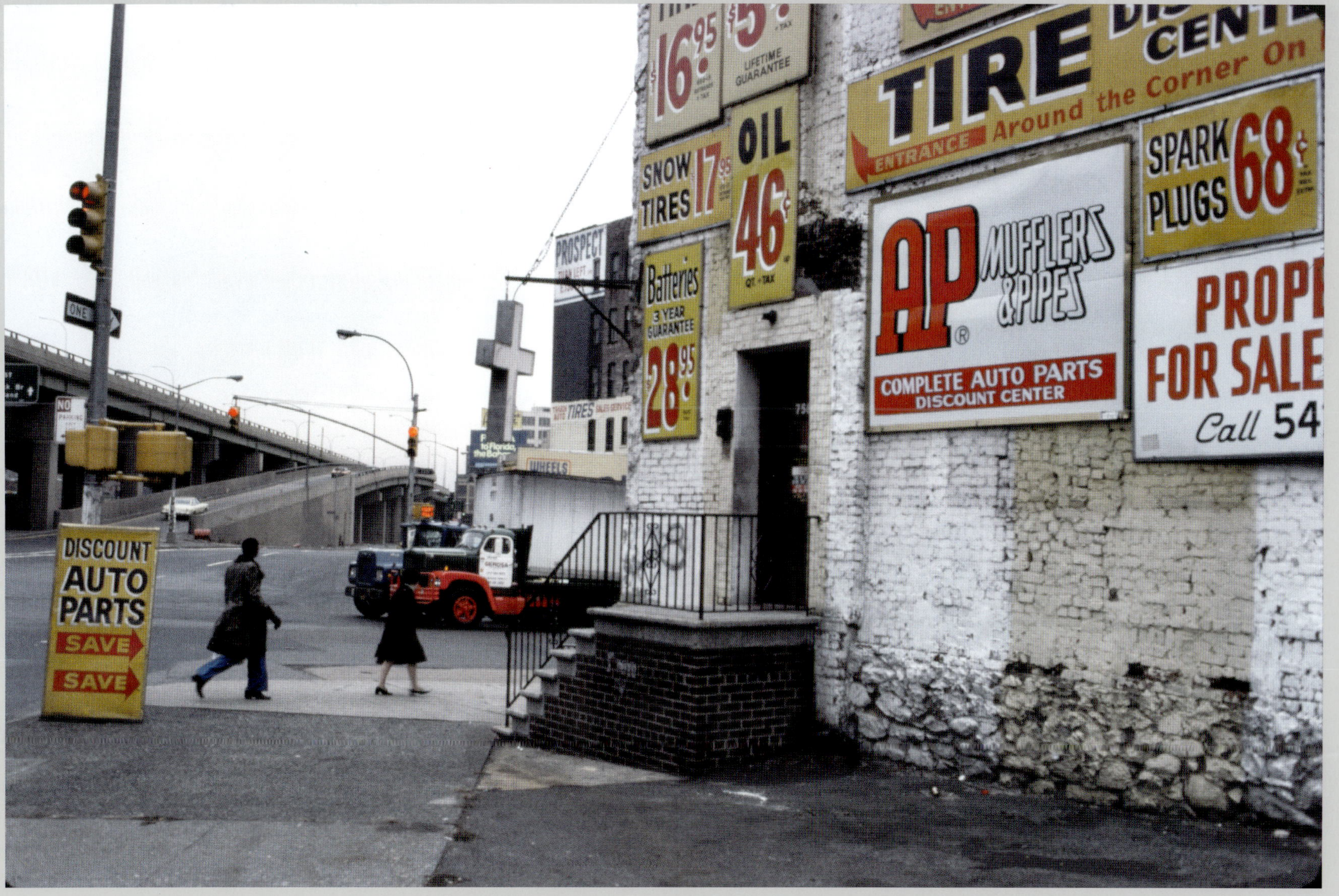
TIRE
ENTRANCE
Around the Corner On
LIFETIME GUARANTEE
SNOW TIRES 17.95
OIL 46¢
QT + TAX
SPARK PLUGS 68¢
Batteries
3 YEAR GUARANTEE
28.95
AP MUFFLERS &PIPES
COMPLETE AUTO PARTS
DISCOUNT CENTER
FOR SALE
Call 54
PROSPECT
ONE
TIRES
WHEELS
DISCOUNT AUTO PARTS
SAVE
SAVE

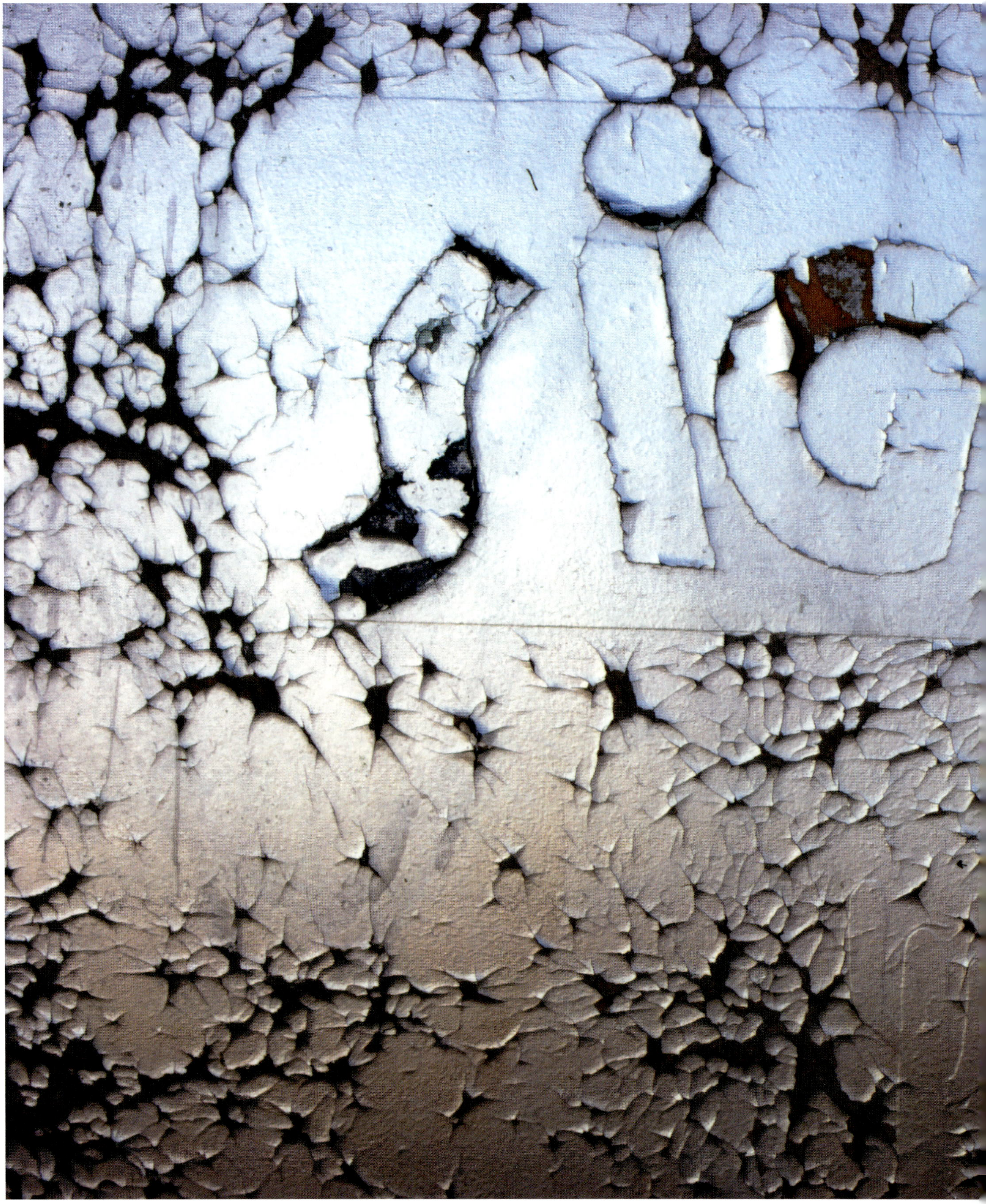

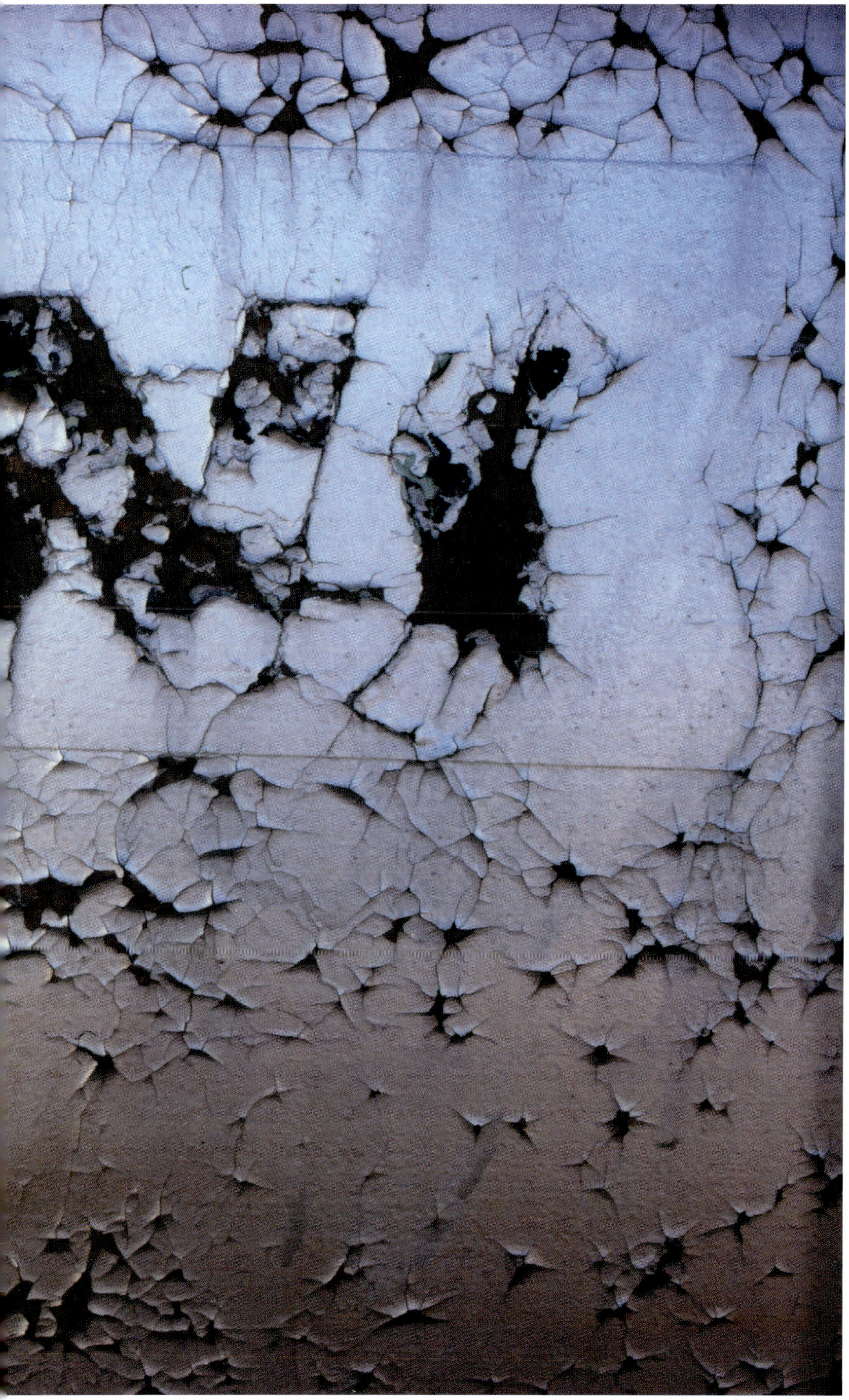

Panel of Sign Painter's Truck, n.d.

New Haven Green, May Day, 1970
Allen Ginsberg, Jerry Rubin, Abbie Hoffman
with an unidentified woman

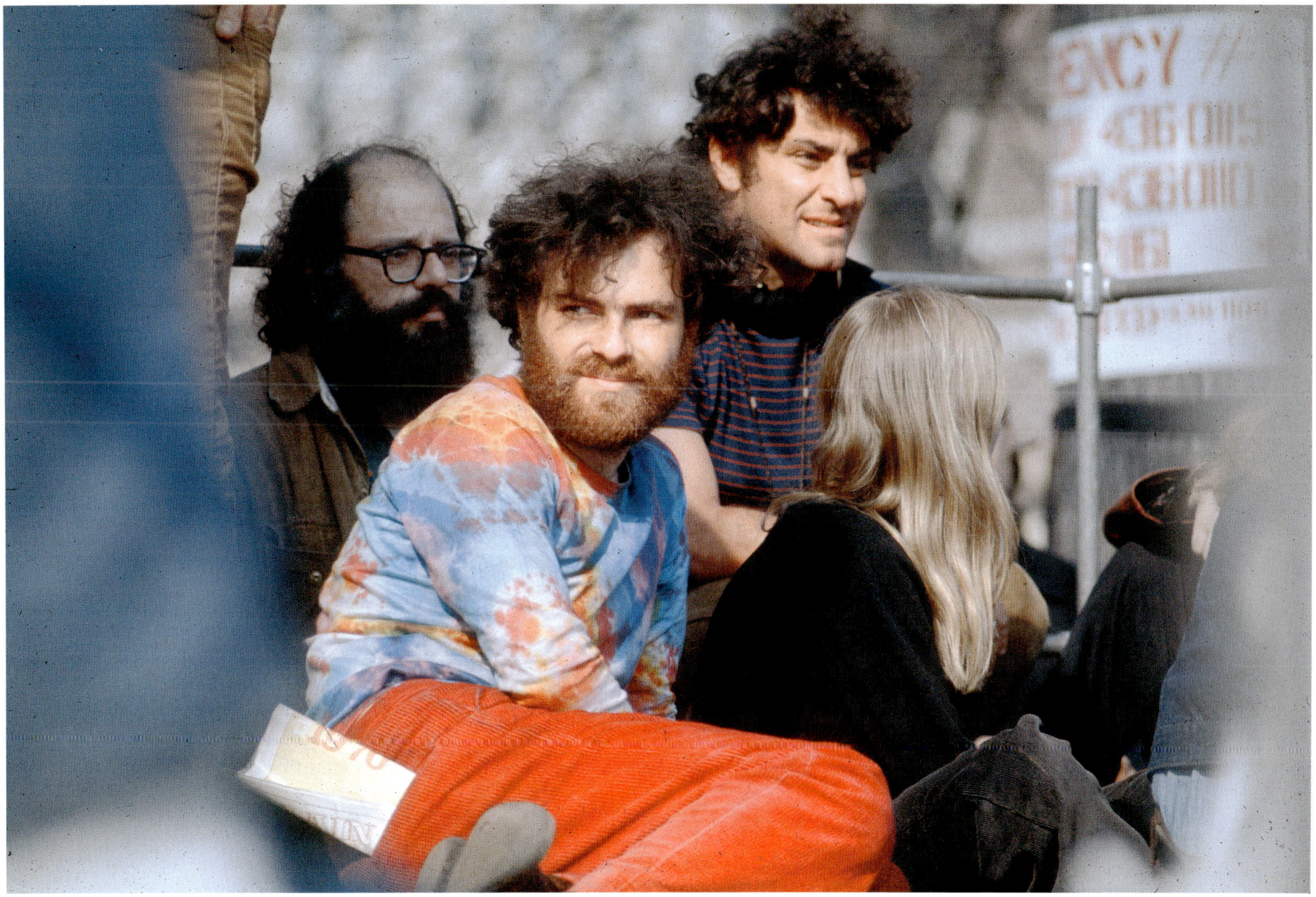
ENCY

New Haven Green, May Day, 1970

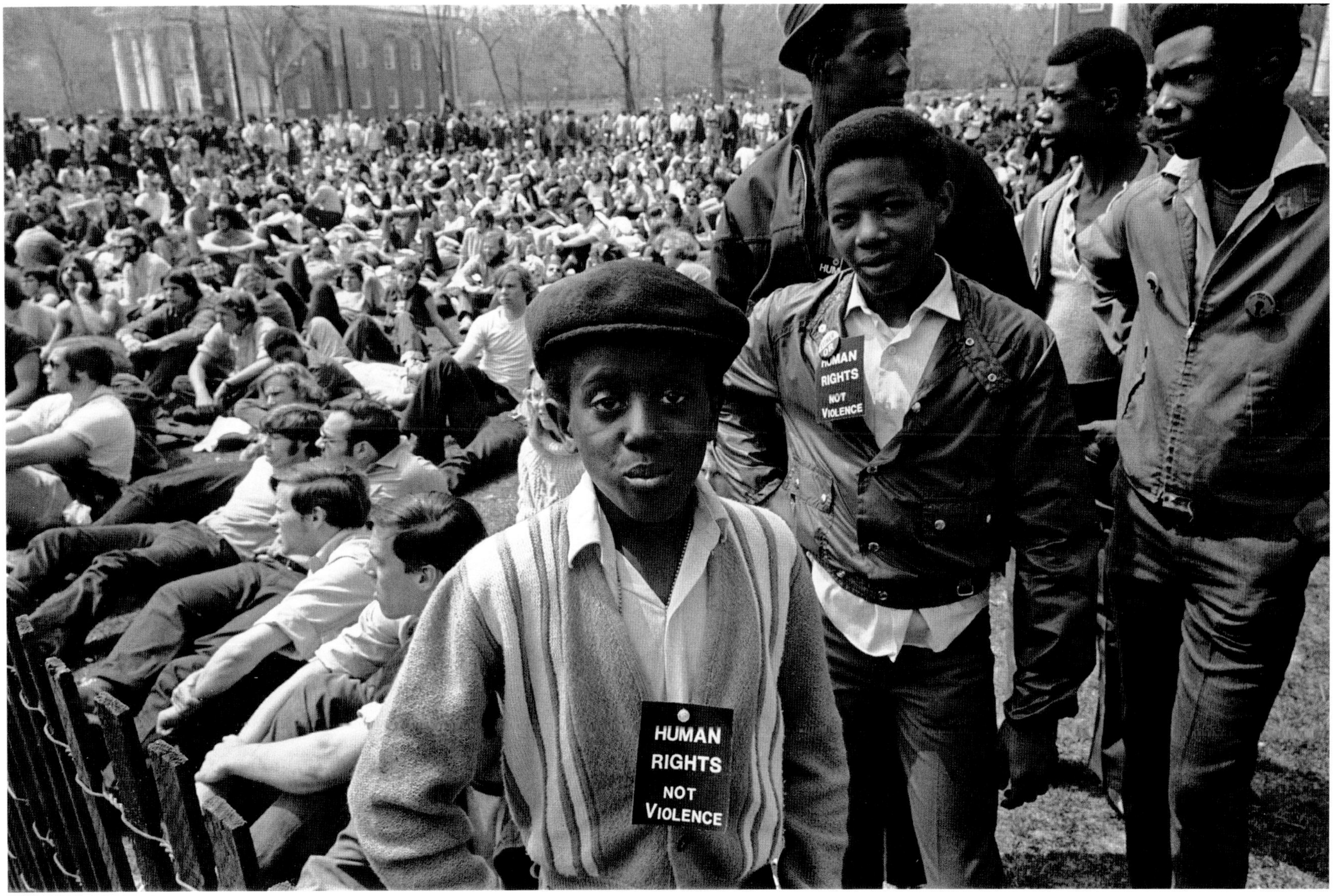
HUMAN
RIGHTS
NOT
VIOLENCE
HUMAN
RIGHTS
NOT
VIOLENCE

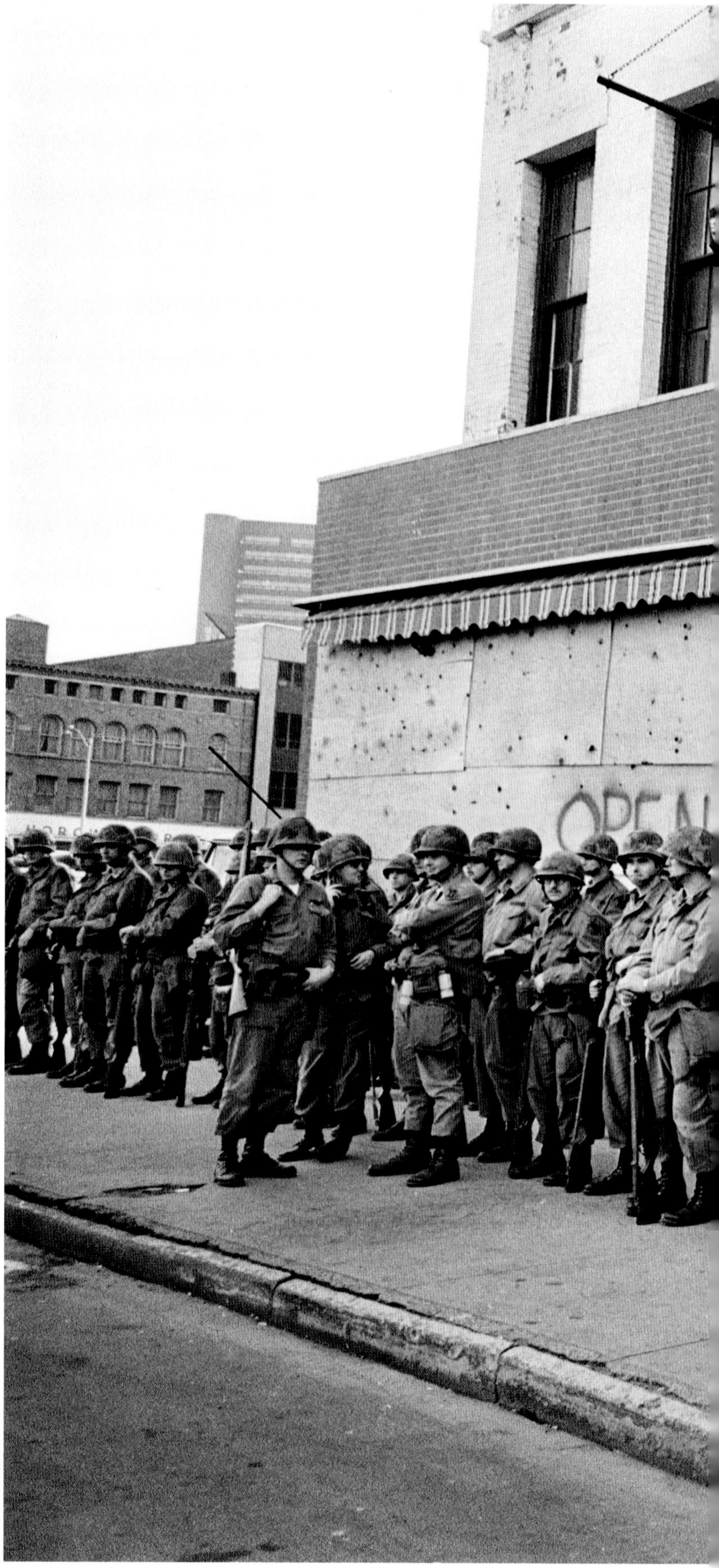

National Guard Troops on the ready, one block from New Haven Green, May Day, 1970

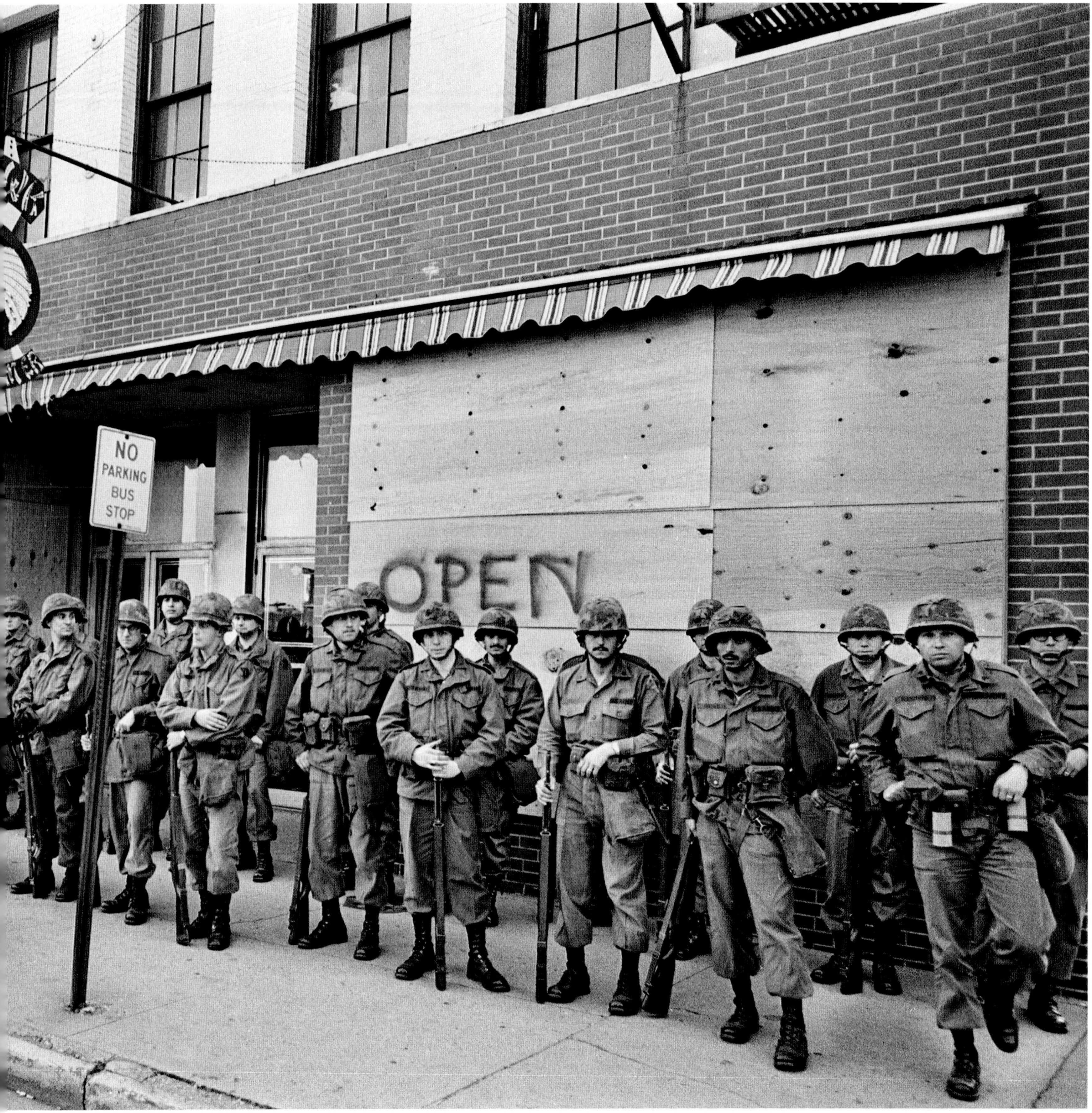
NO
PARKING
BUS
STOP
OPEN

118

Mrs. Bobby Seale, seated just left of center, next to Black Panther Michael Tabor, New Haven Green, May Day, 1970
"Composite"

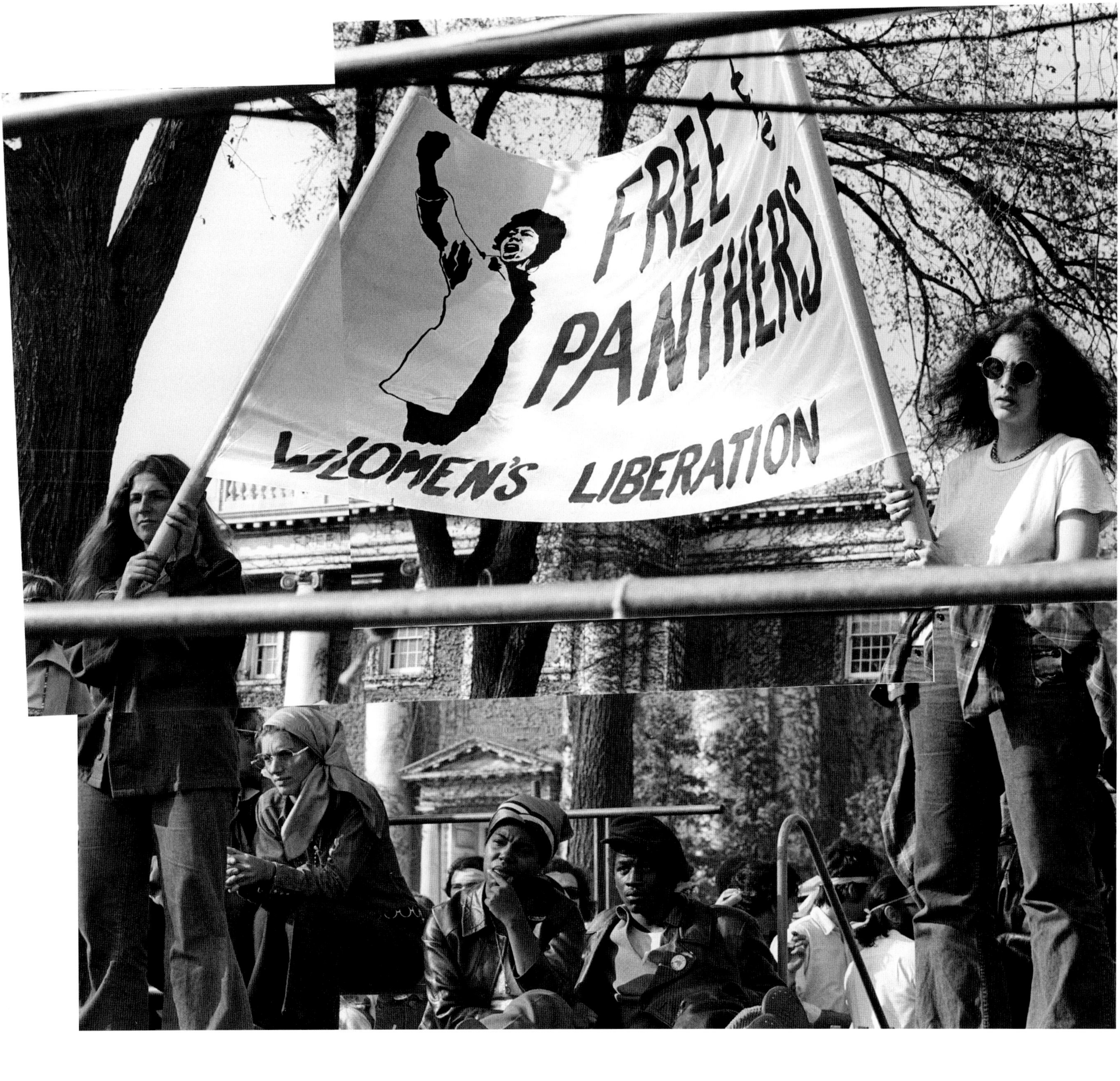
FREE
PANTHERS
WOMEN'S LIBERATION

Store Front, South side of Chapel Street near intersection of College Street, New Haven, Connecticut

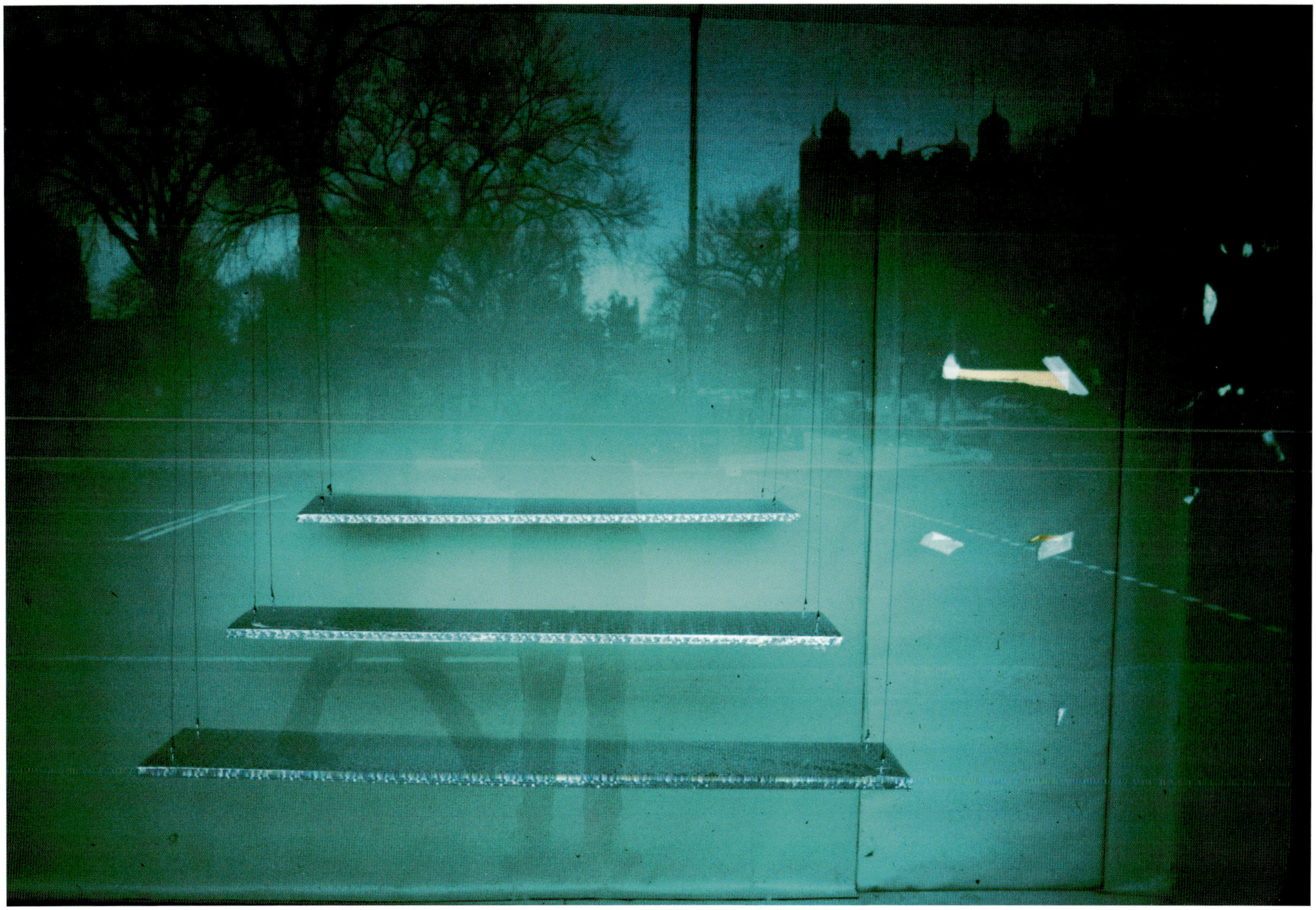

122

Exiting Lincoln Tunnel, Southbound, 2019

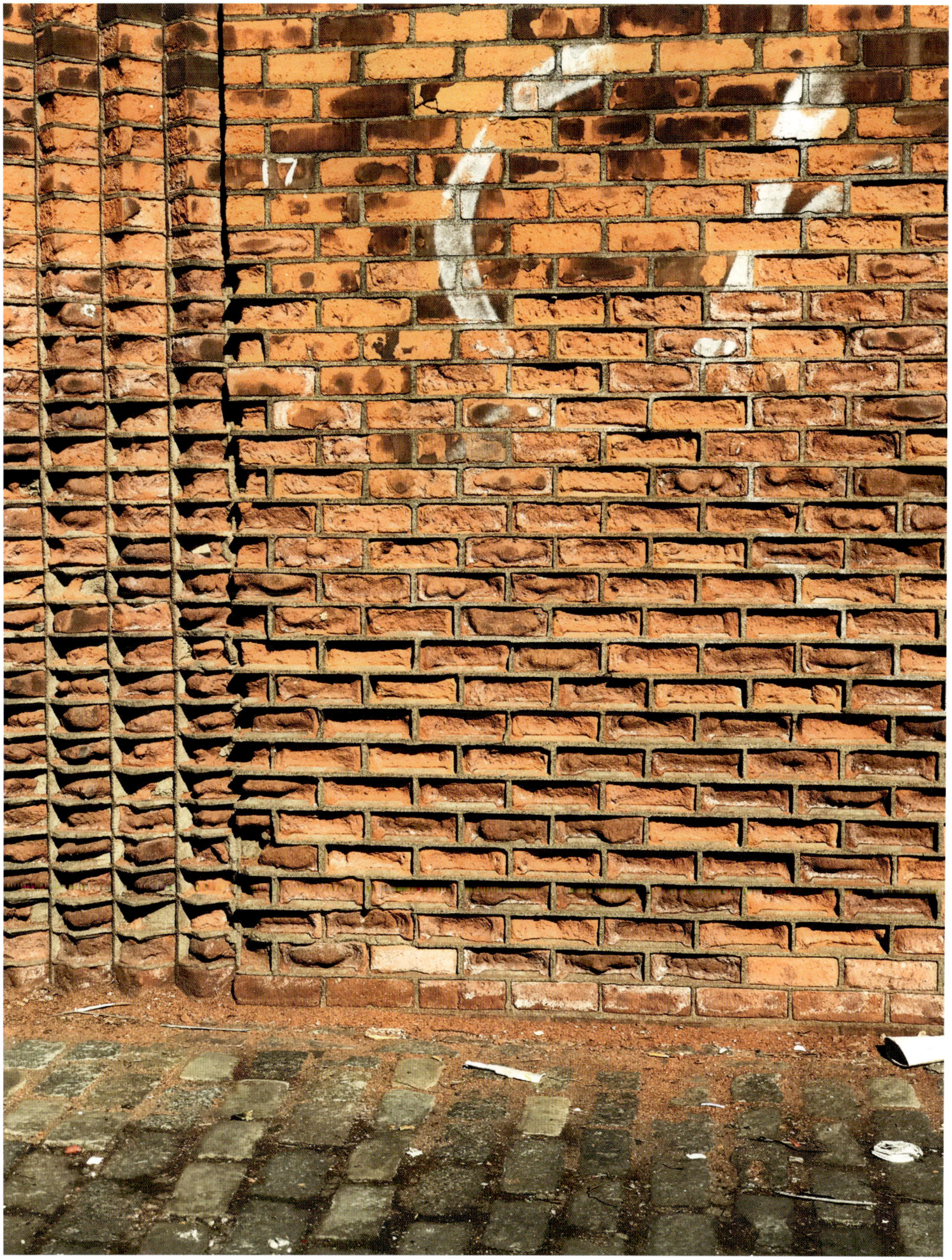
17

South Side of Tandoor Restaurant, New Haven, Connecticut, 2020

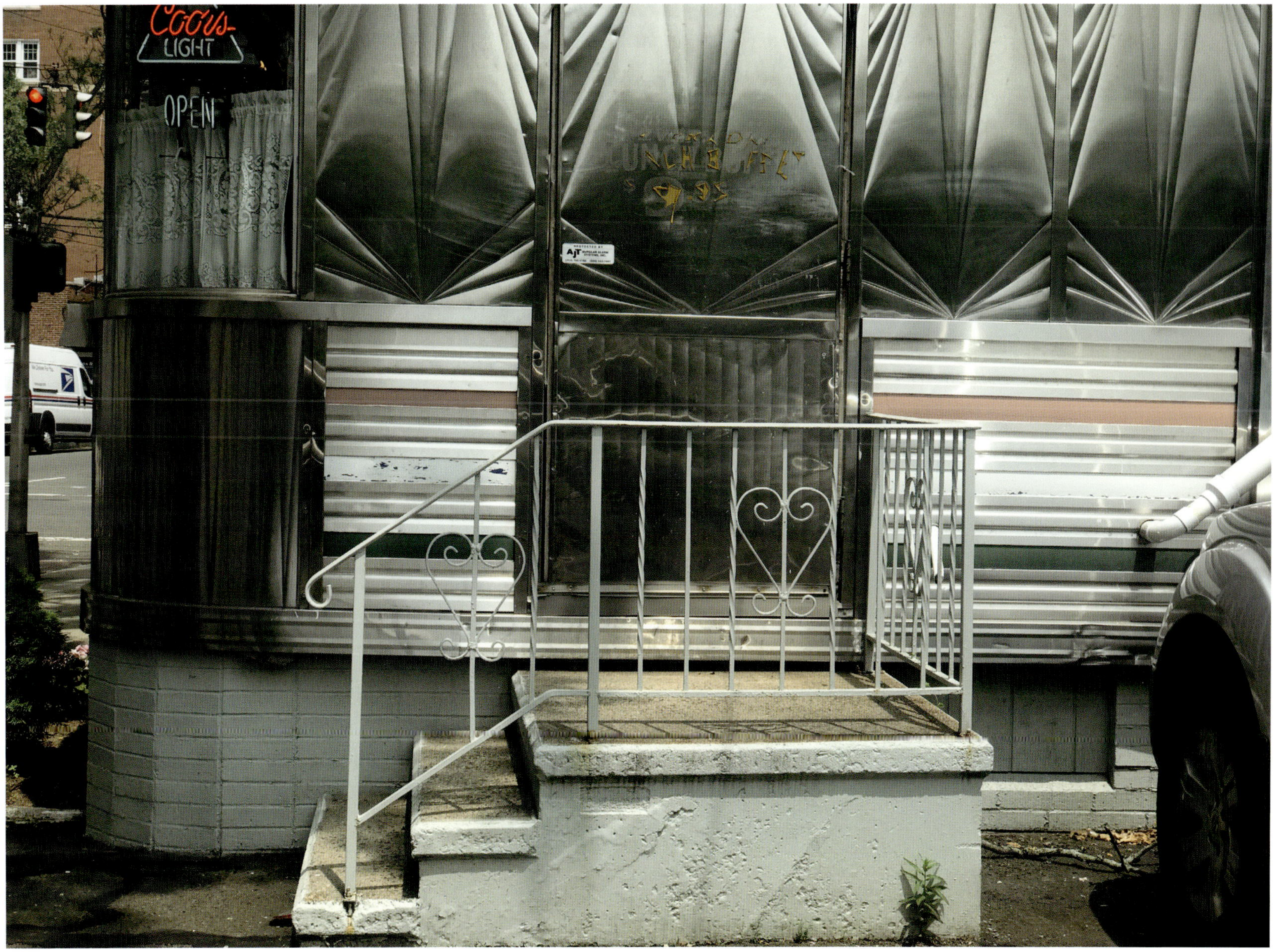
Coors
LIGHT
OPEN

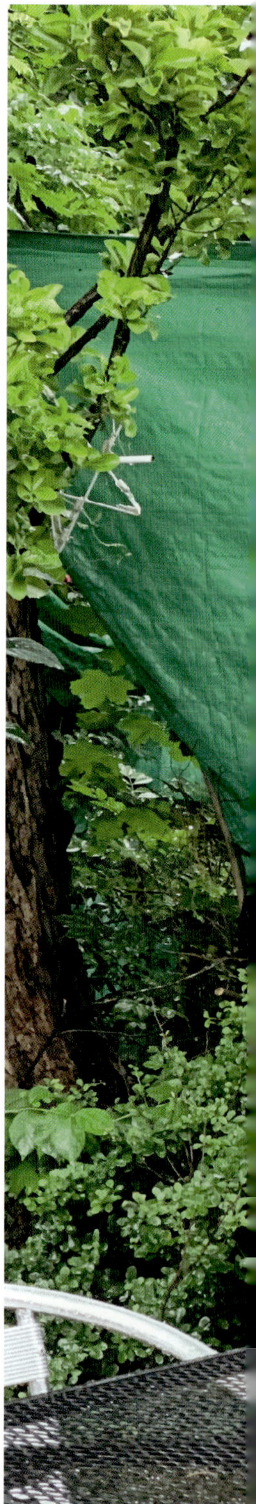

Kasbah Garden Cafe, New Haven, Connecticut 2022

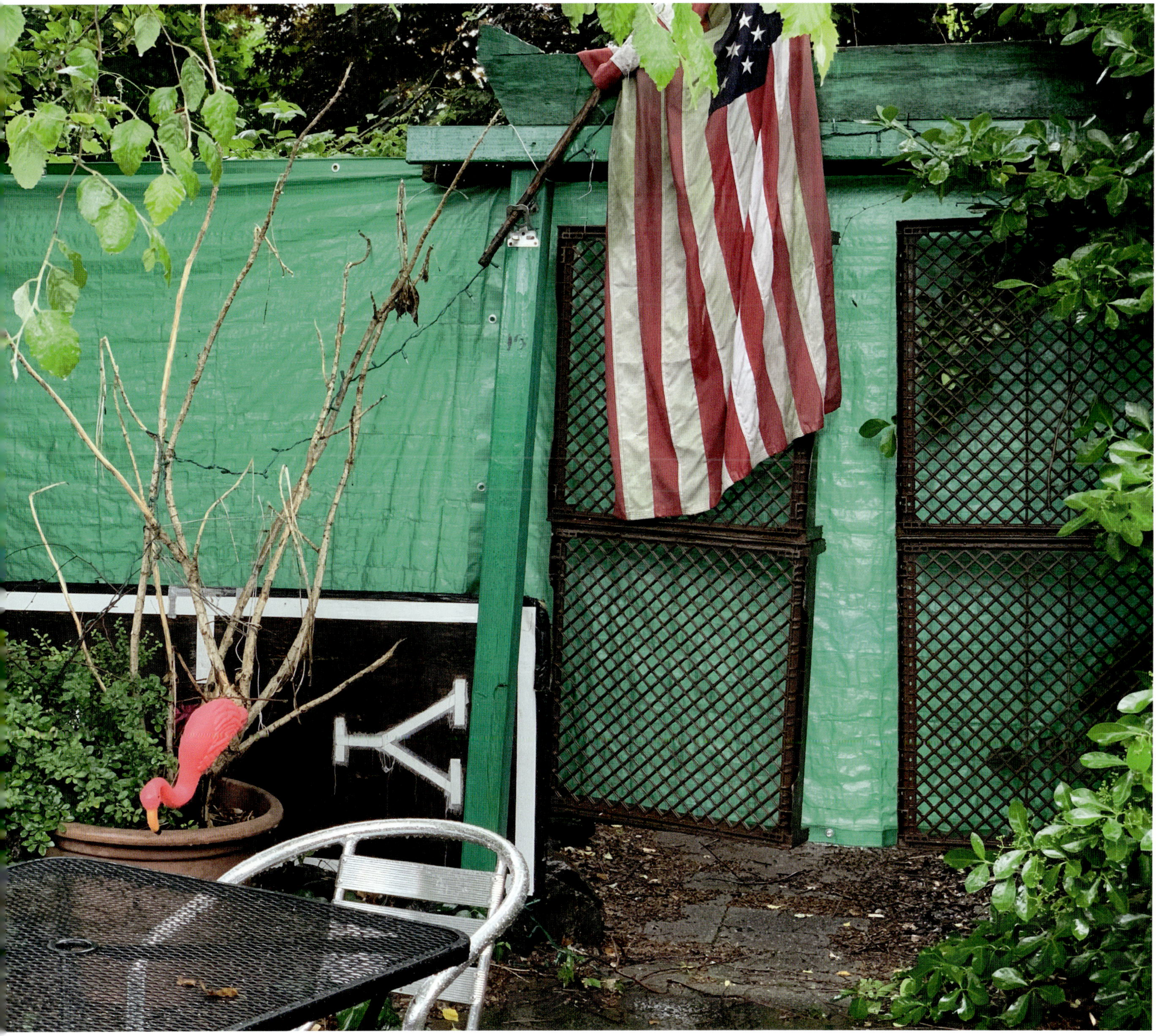
Y

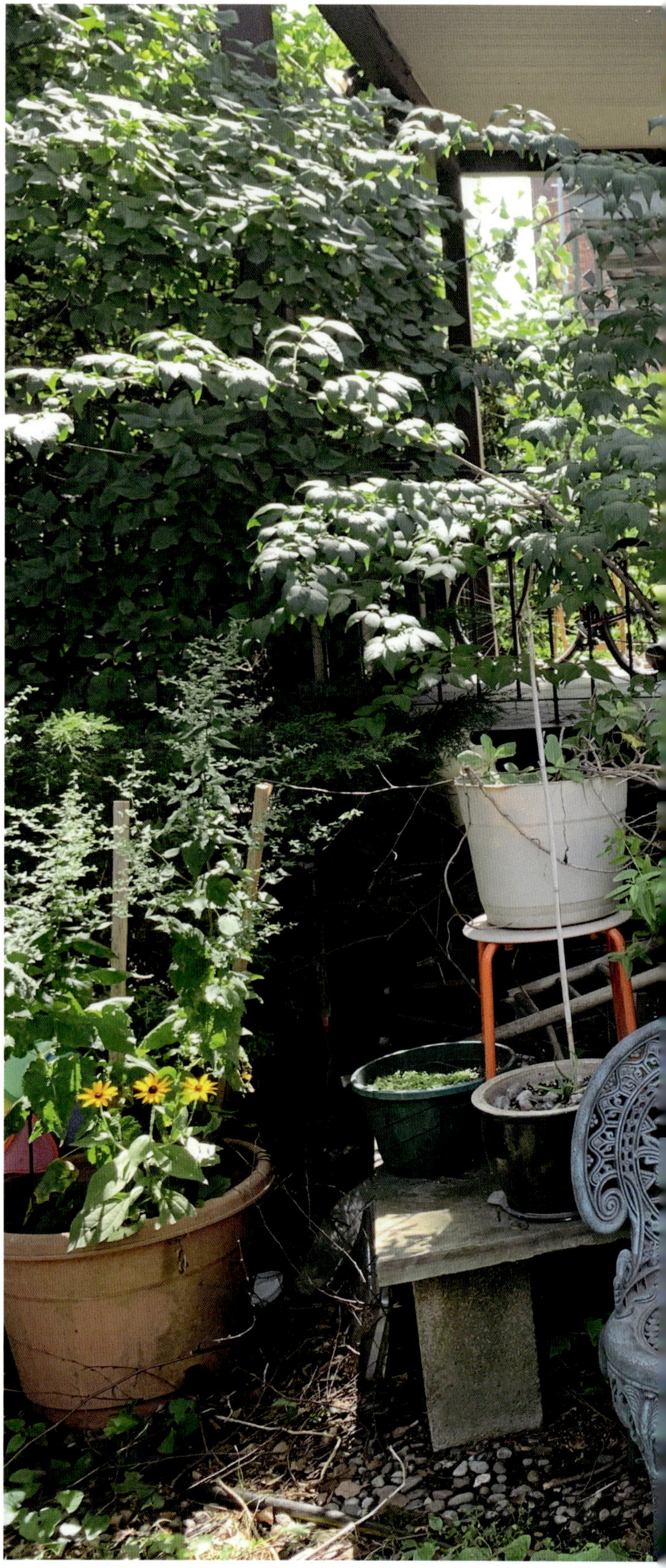

Kasbah Garden Cafe, New Haven, Connecticut 2021

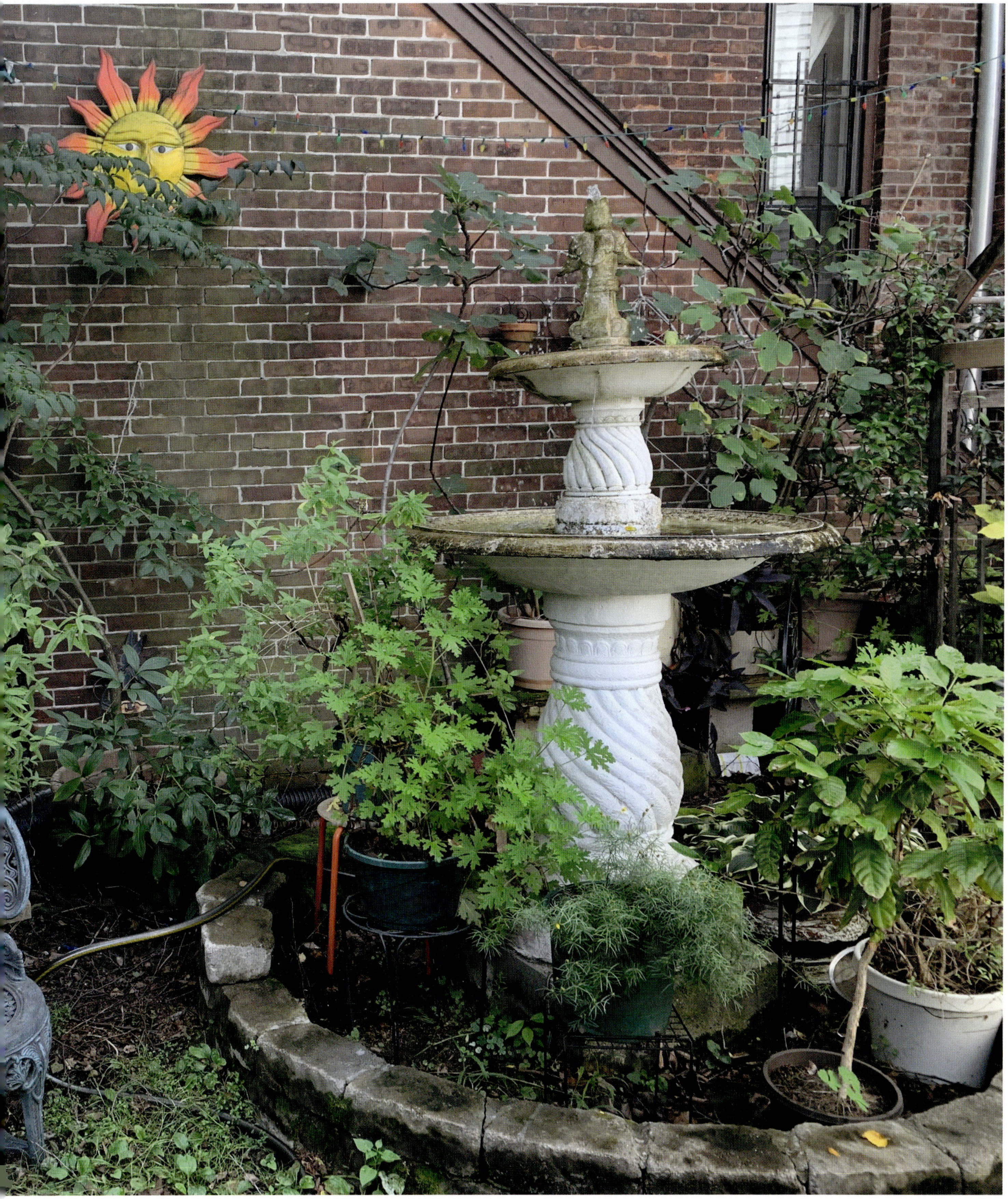

Untitled, Bethany, CT, 2018

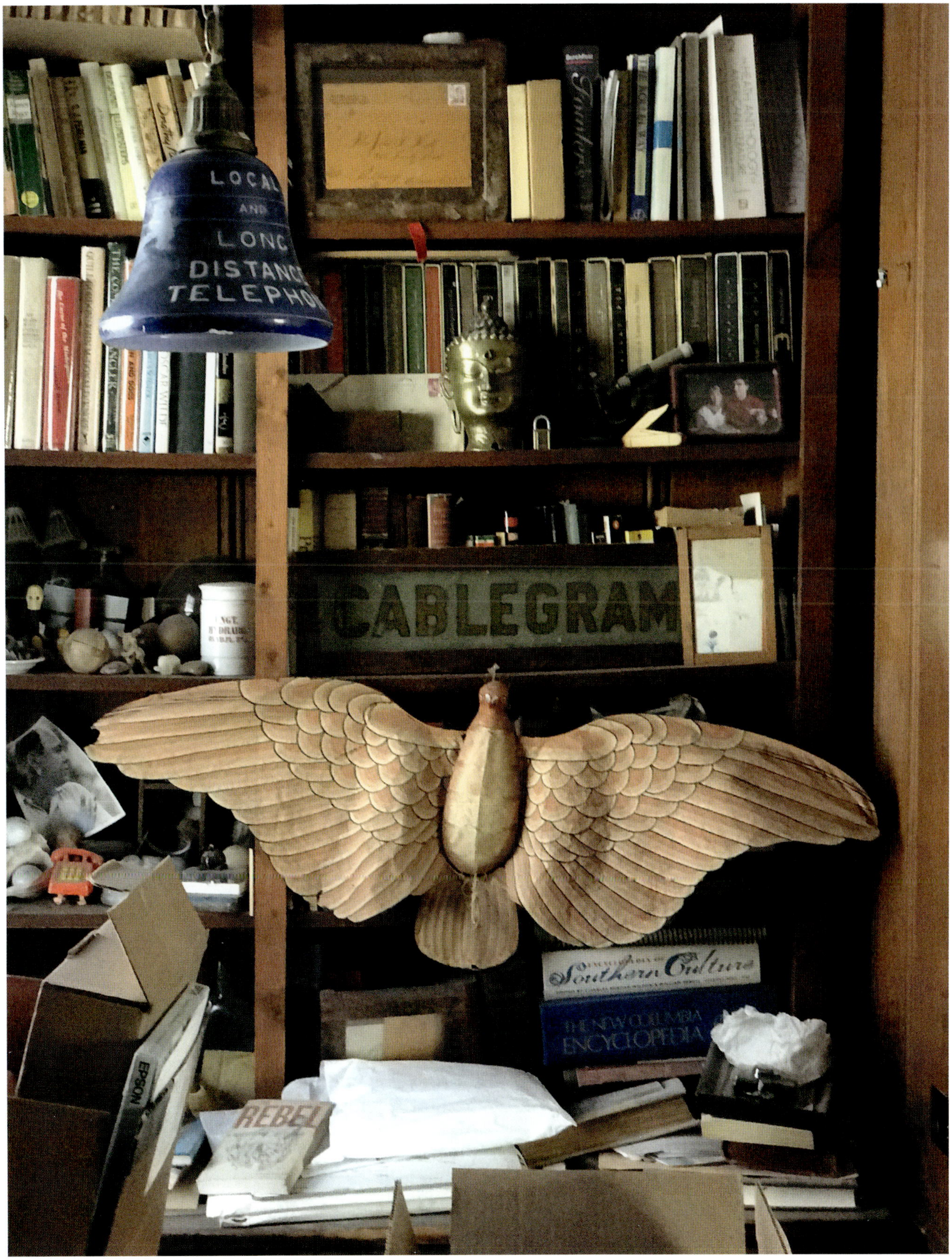
LOCAL
AND
LONG
DISTANC
TELEPHO
CABLEGRAM
Southern Culture
THE NEW COLUMBIA
ENCYCLOPEDIA
EPSON
REBEL

Untitled, Arm & Hammer Baking Soda Bird Cards, 2021

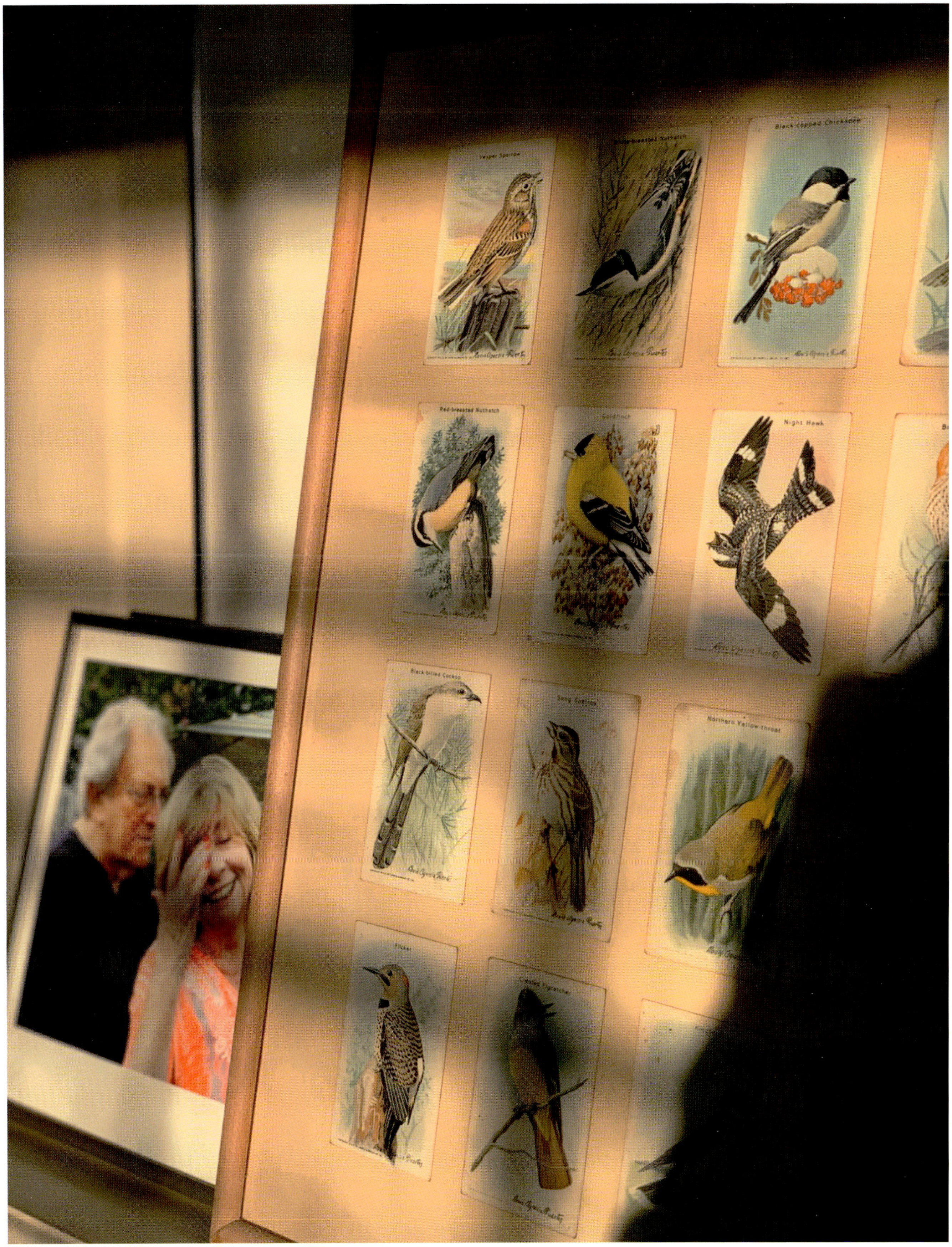
Vesper Sparrow
Black-capped Chickadee
Red-breasted Nuthatch
Goldfinch
Night Hawk
Black-billed Cuckoo
Song Sparrow
Northern Yellow-throat
Flicker
Crested Flycatcher

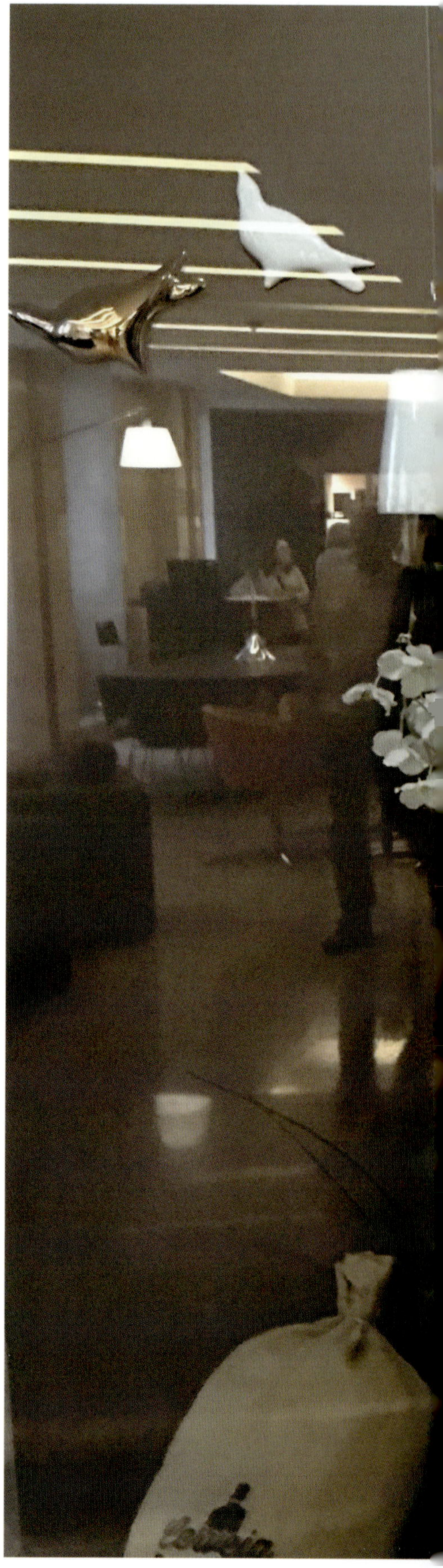

Lobby, Hotel Mercure, Porto, Portugal, 2018

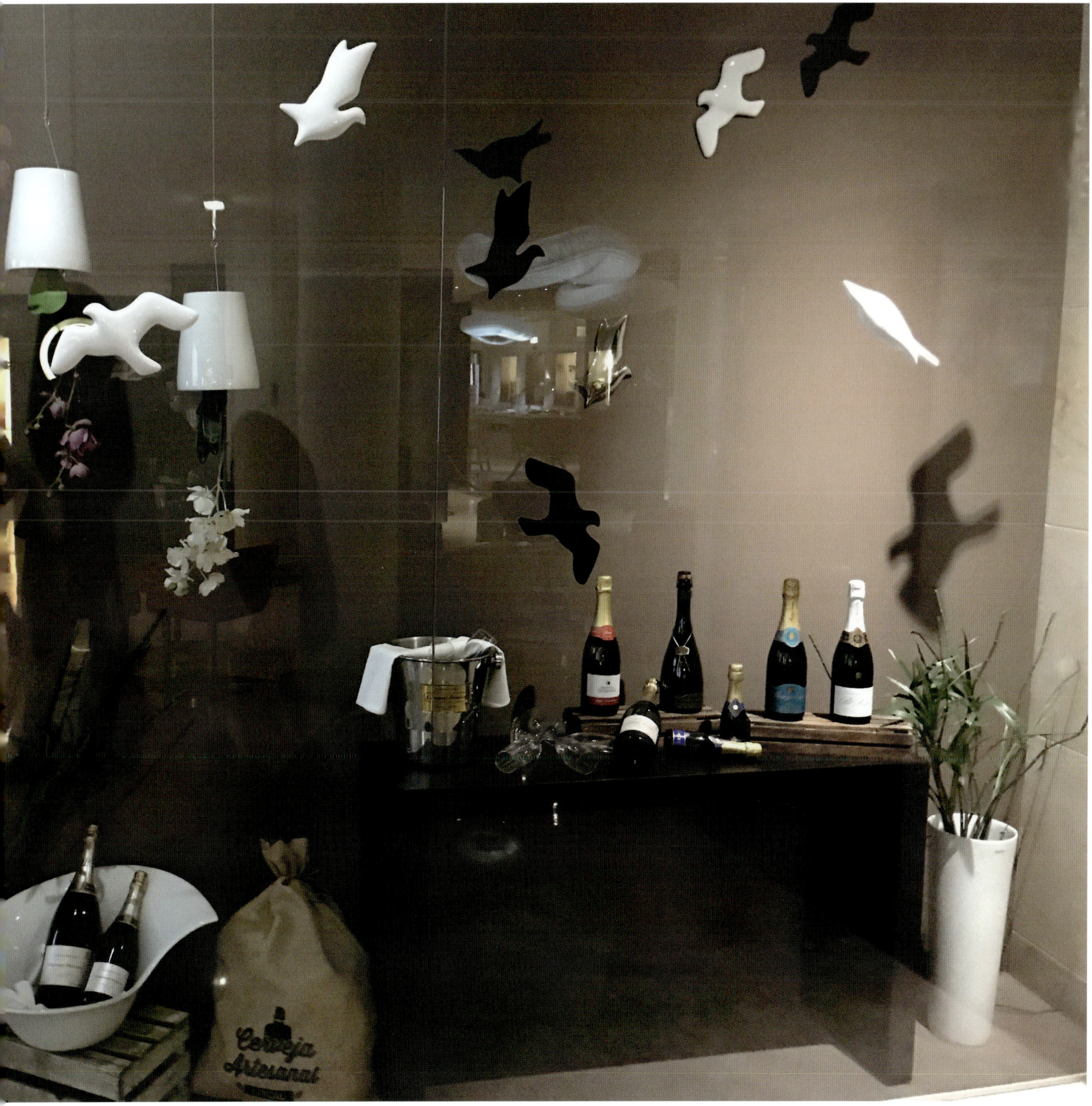
Cerveja
Artesanal

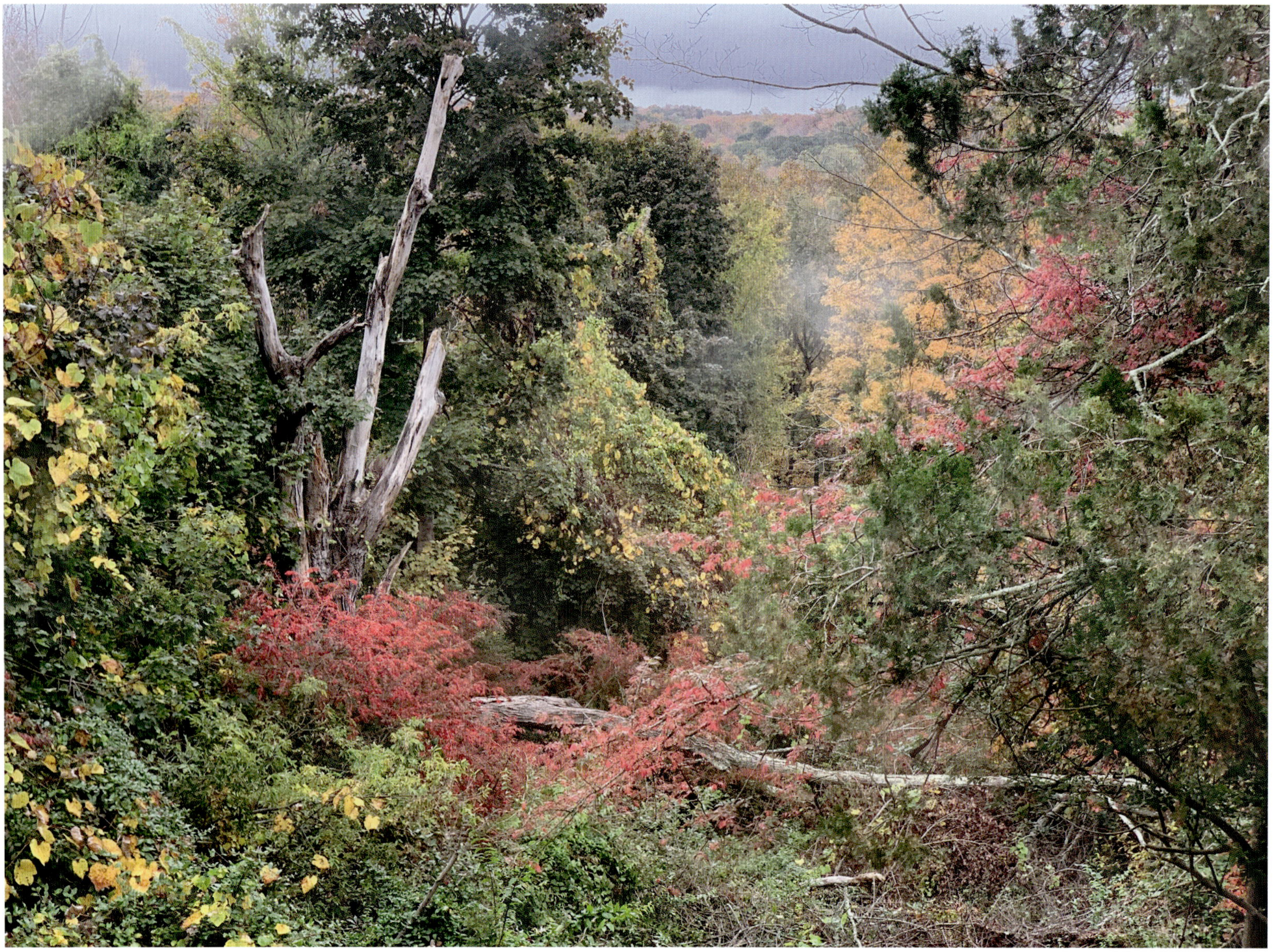

Bethany, Connecticut, View from Amity Road, October 2020, January 2021

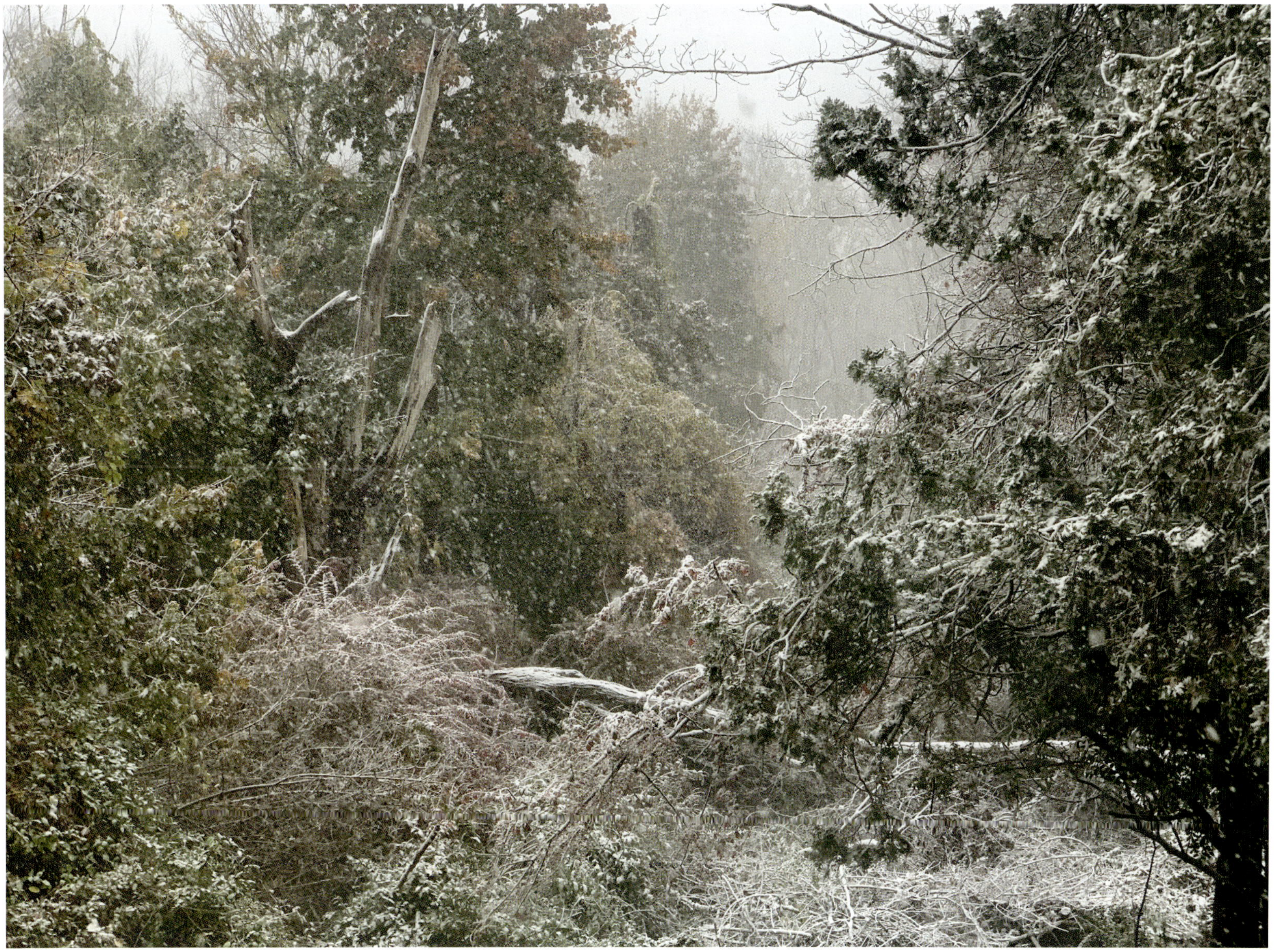

Untitled, Bethany, Connecticut, 2018

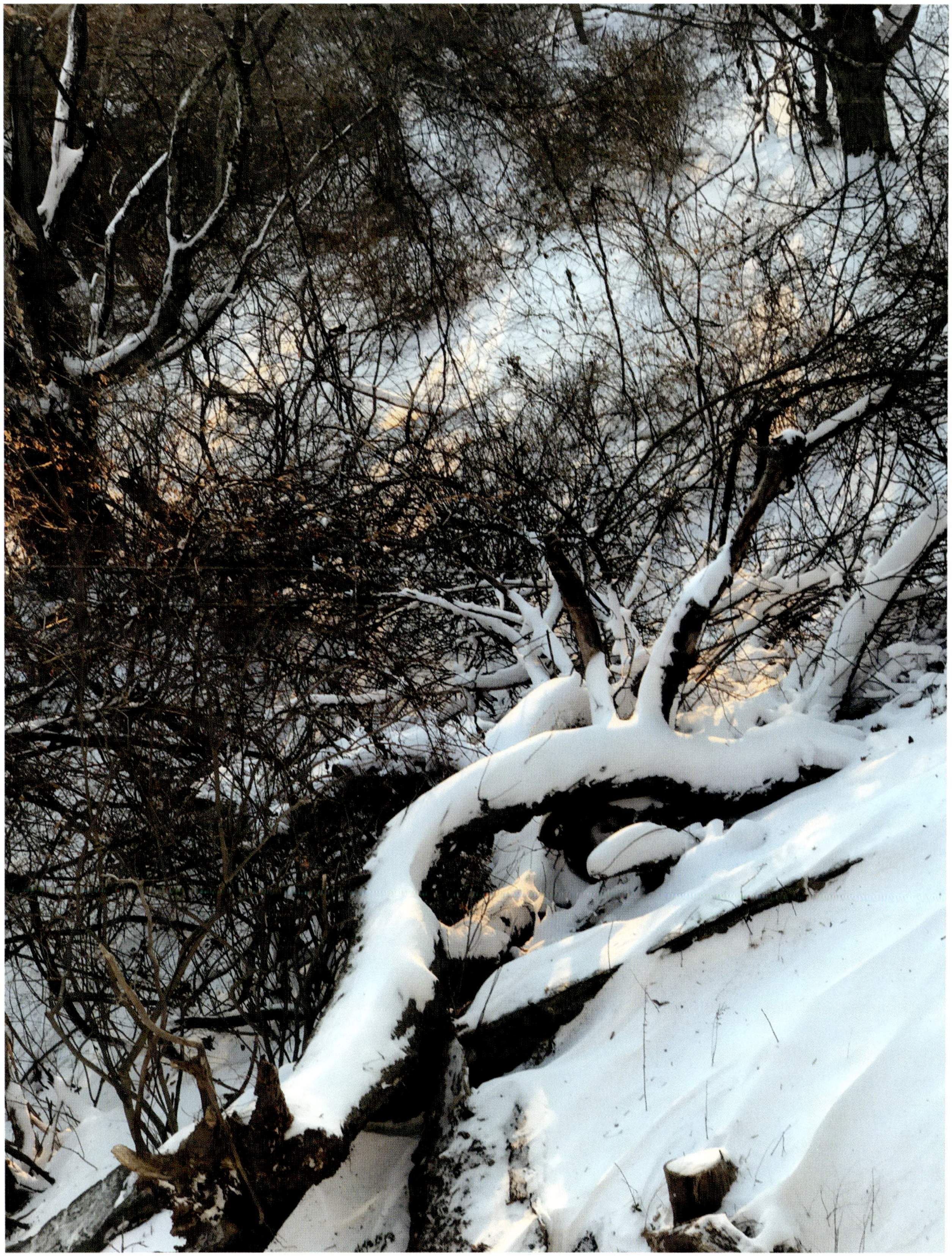

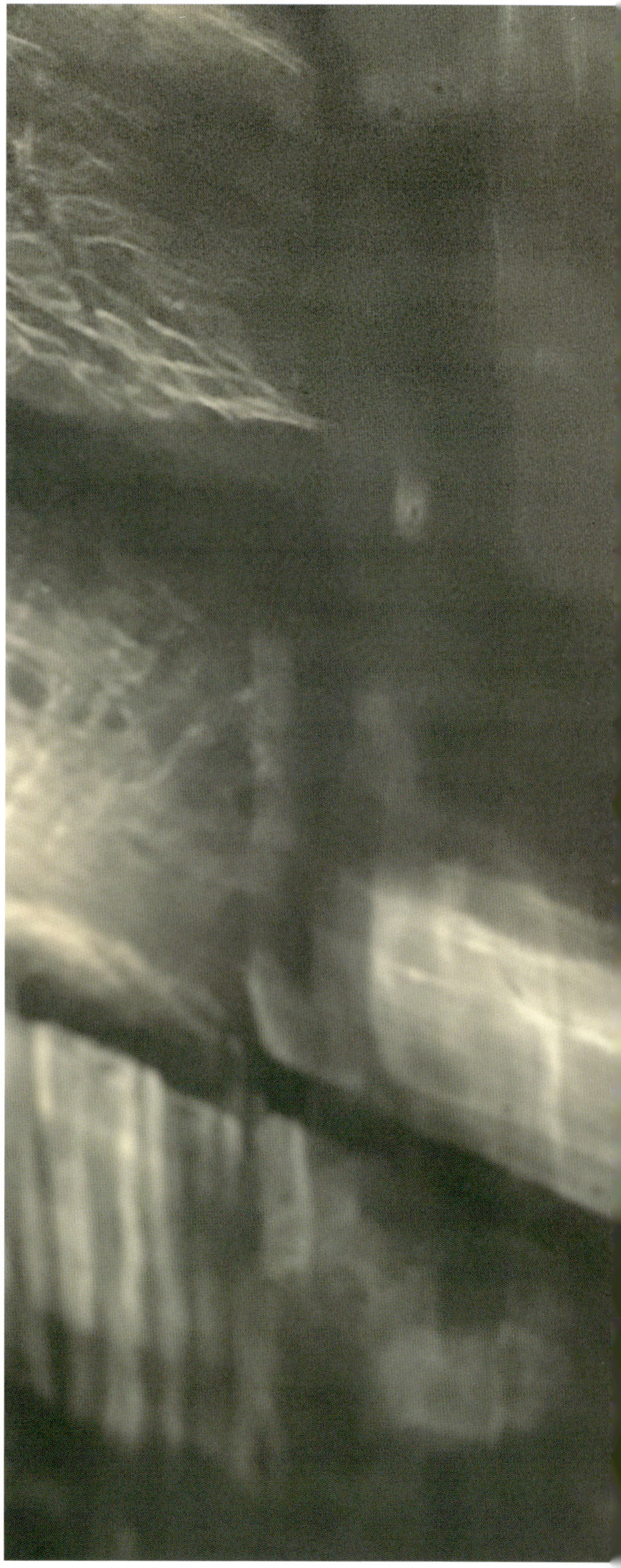

Untitled, New Haven, Connecticut, 2022

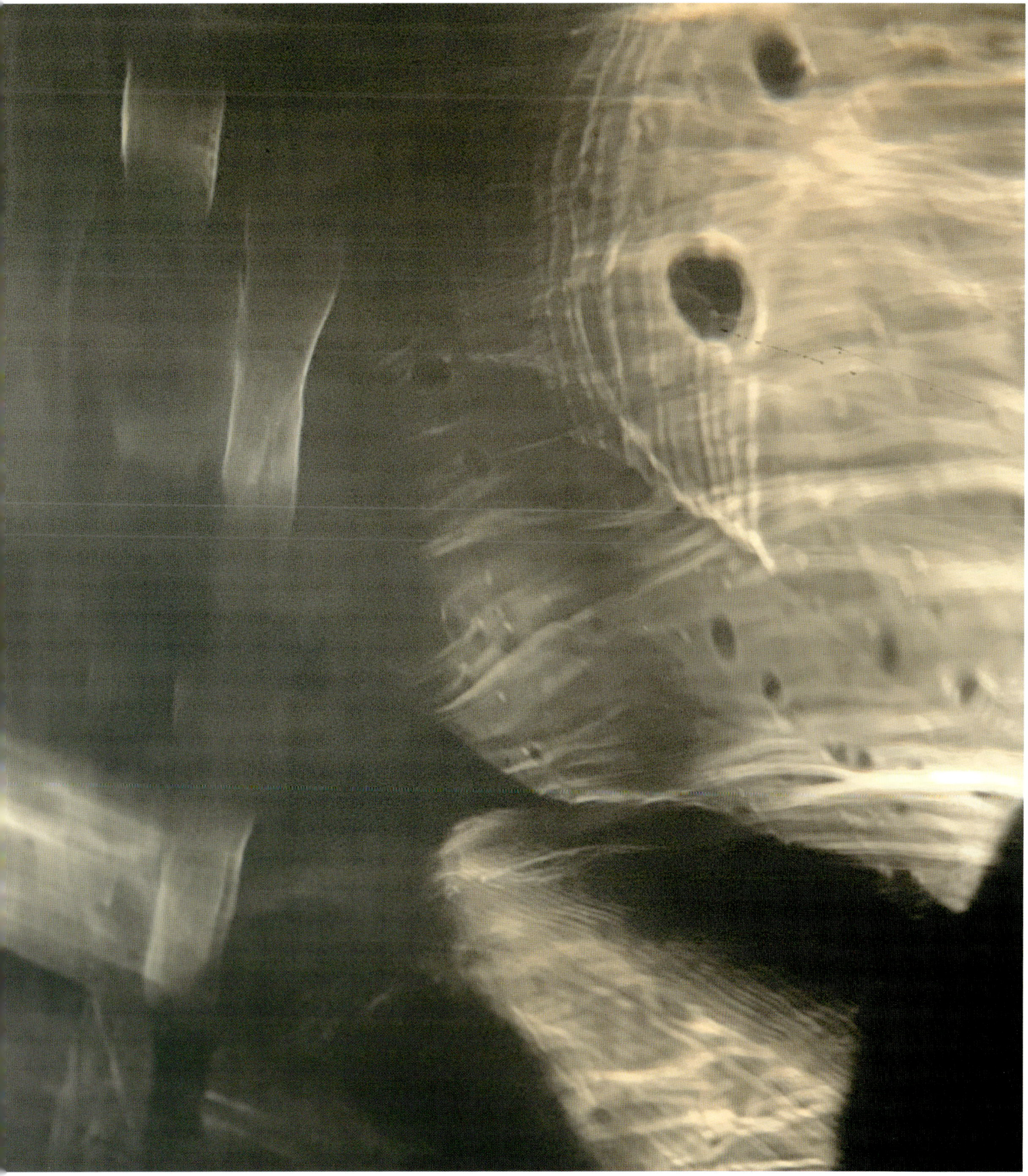

Water in Concavity, Driveway, 2018

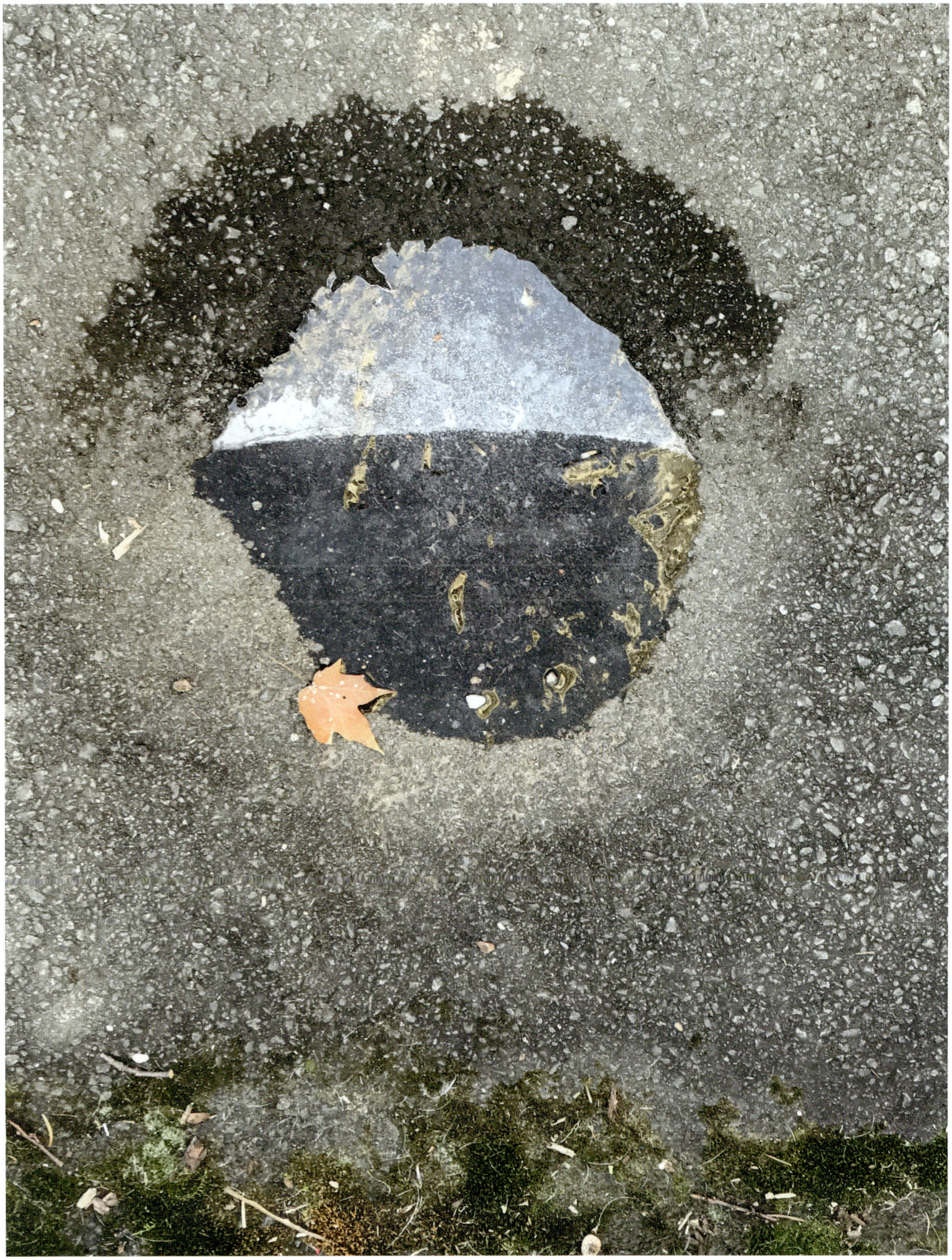

Asphalt Patterns, 2018

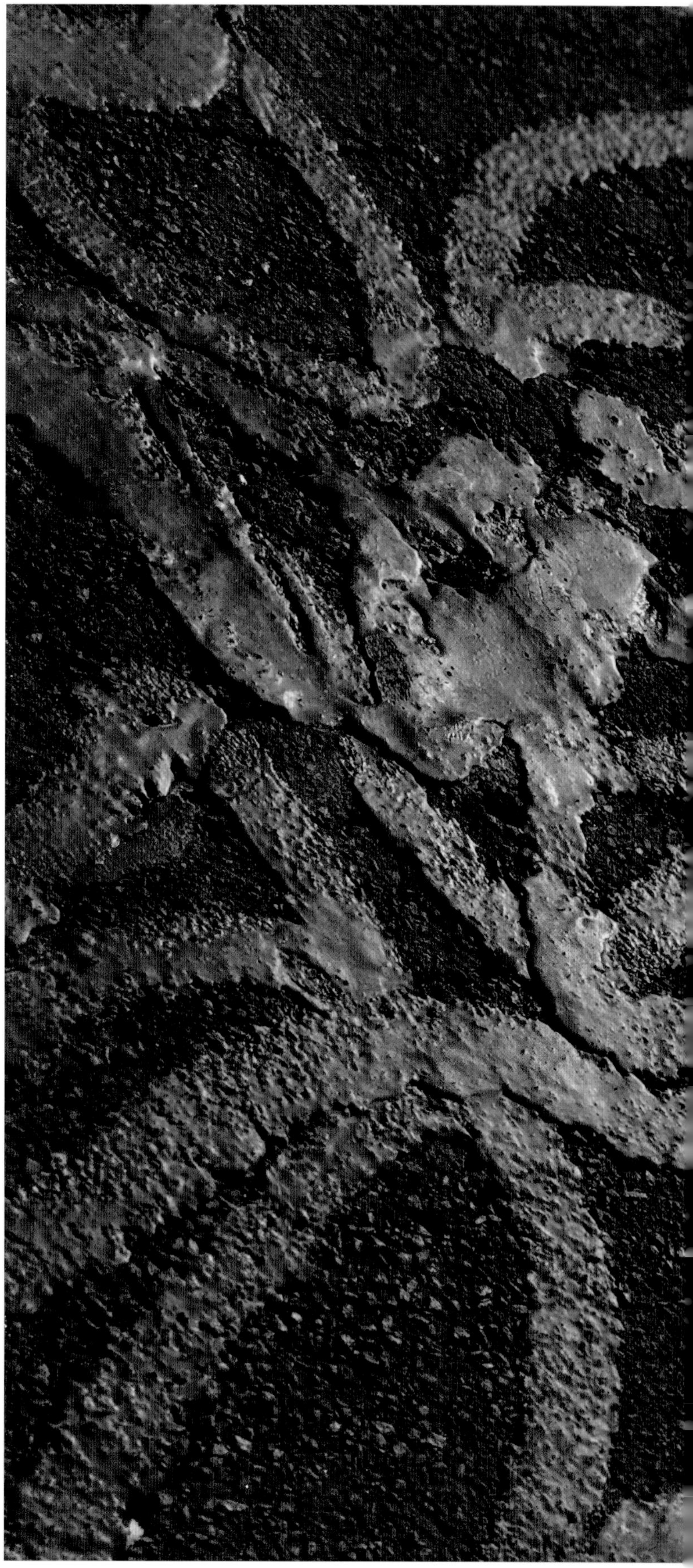

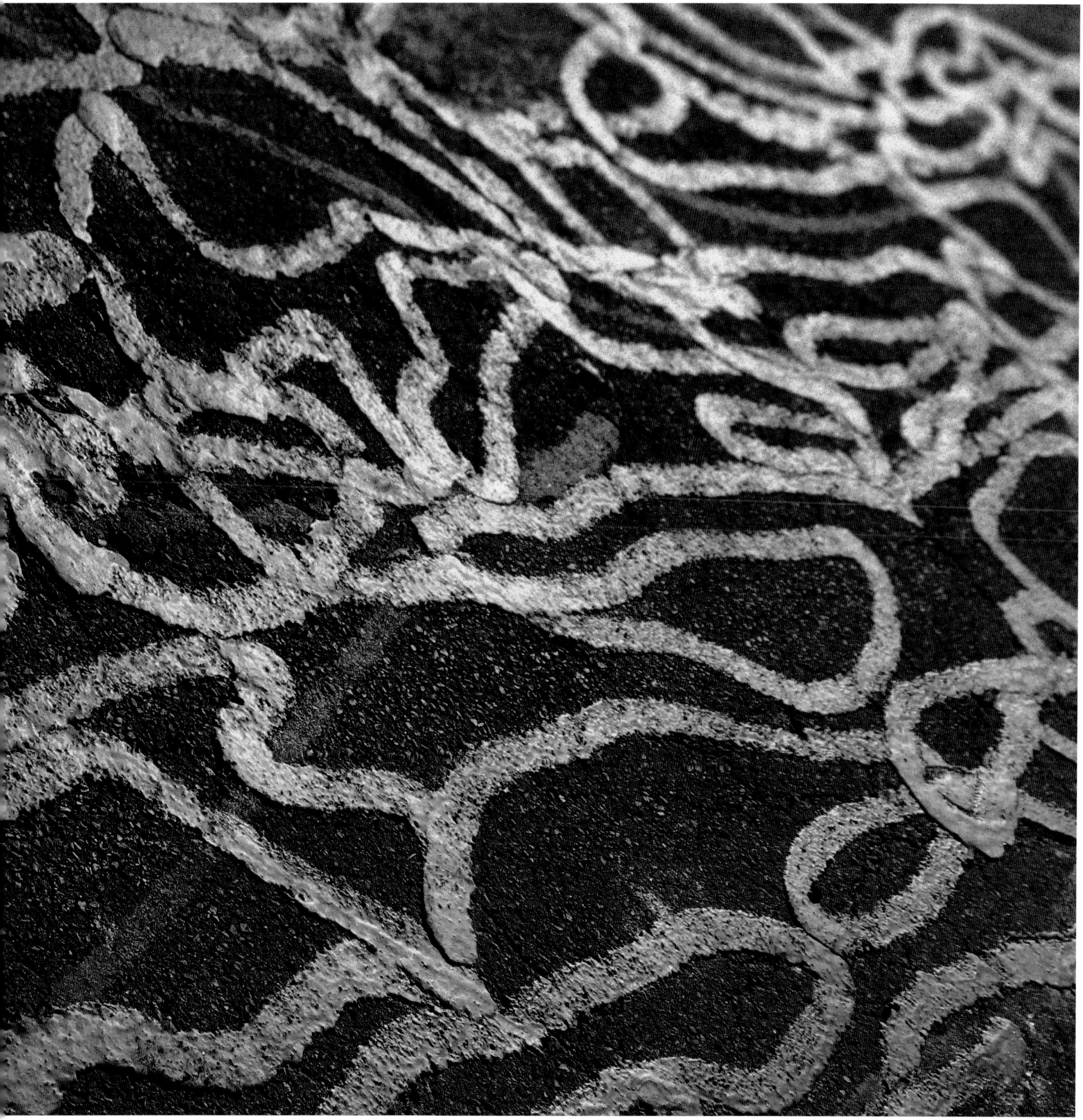

Diner, Bethany, Connecticut, 2022

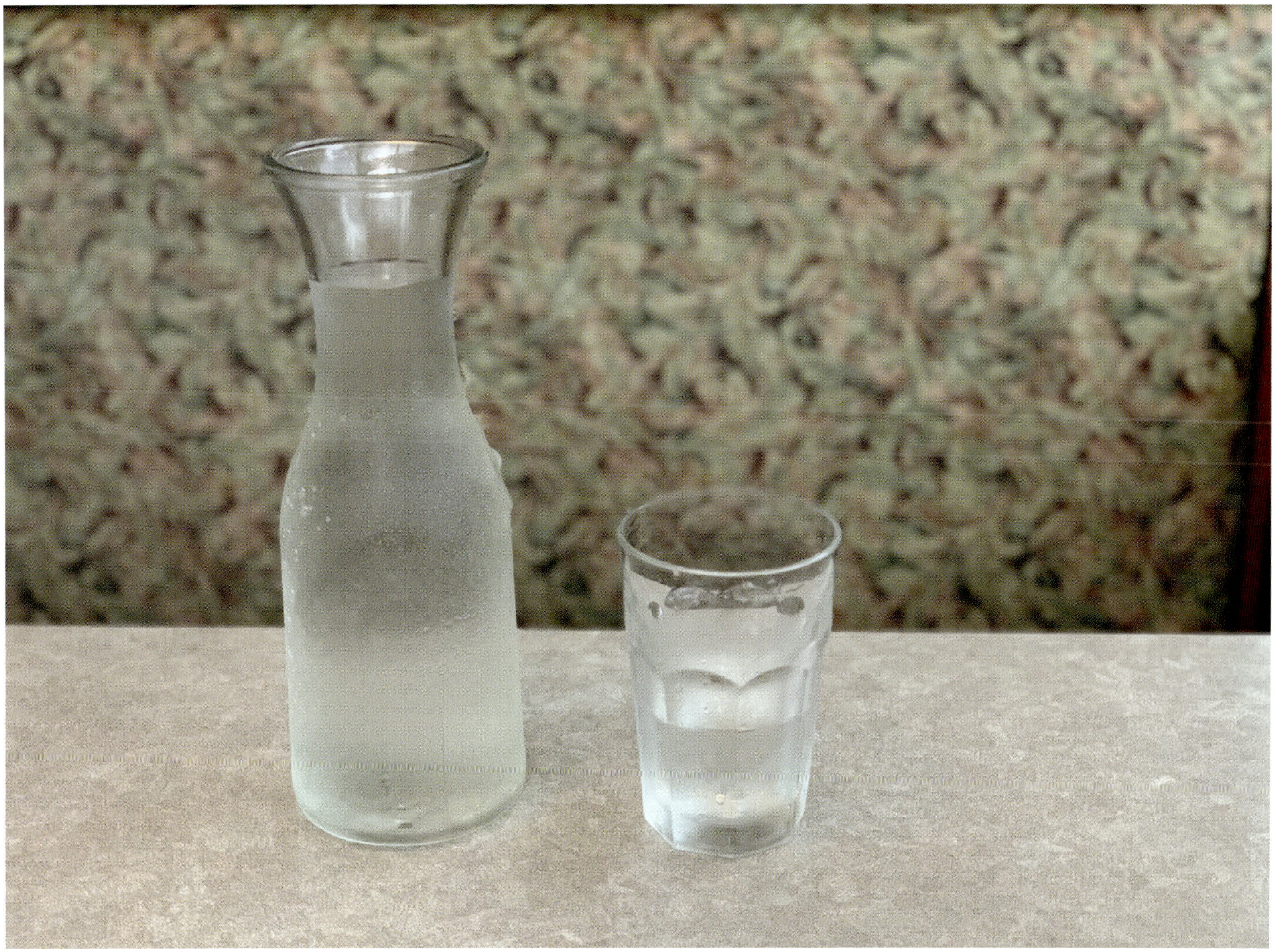

Amity Diner, New Haven, Connecticut, 2021

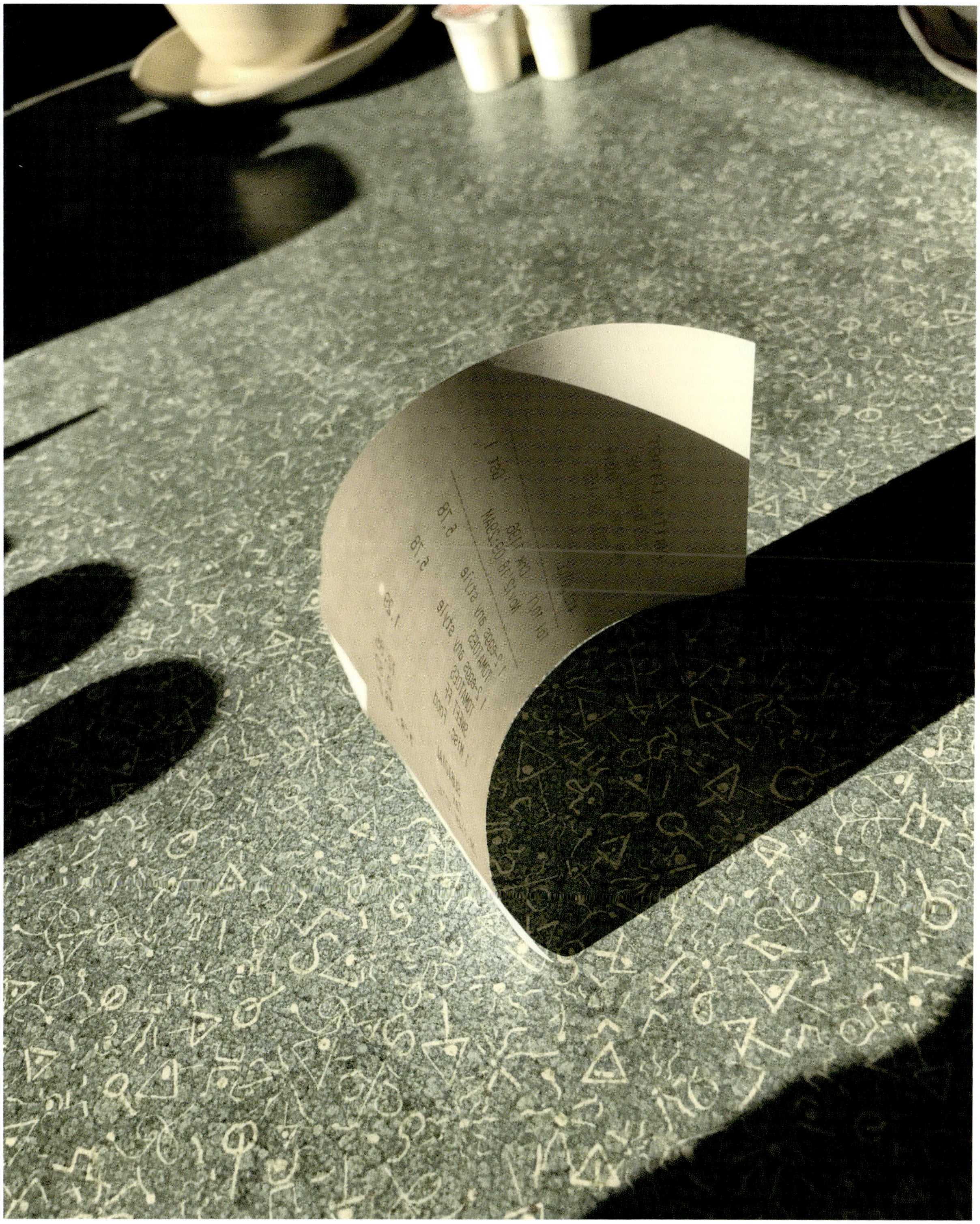

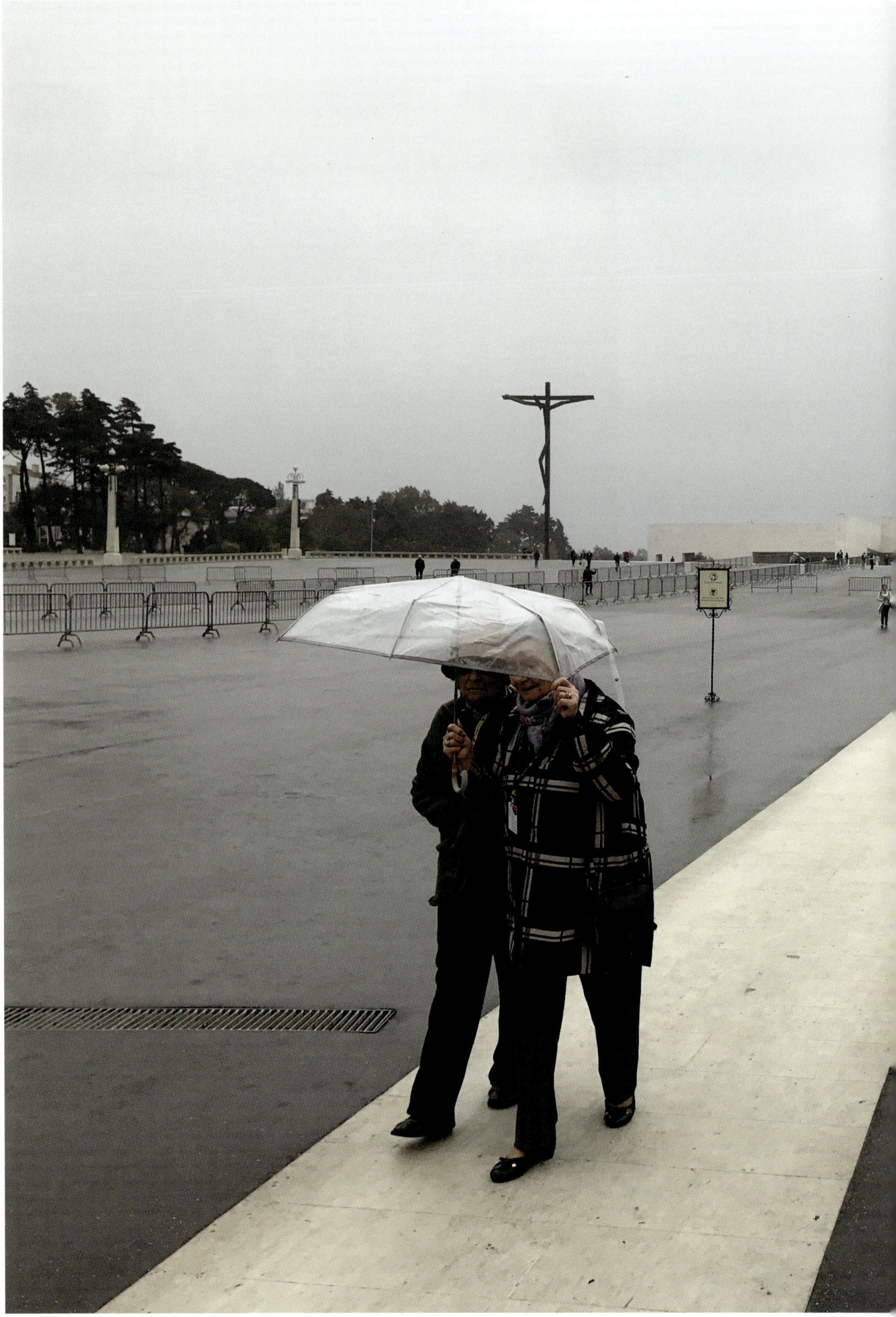

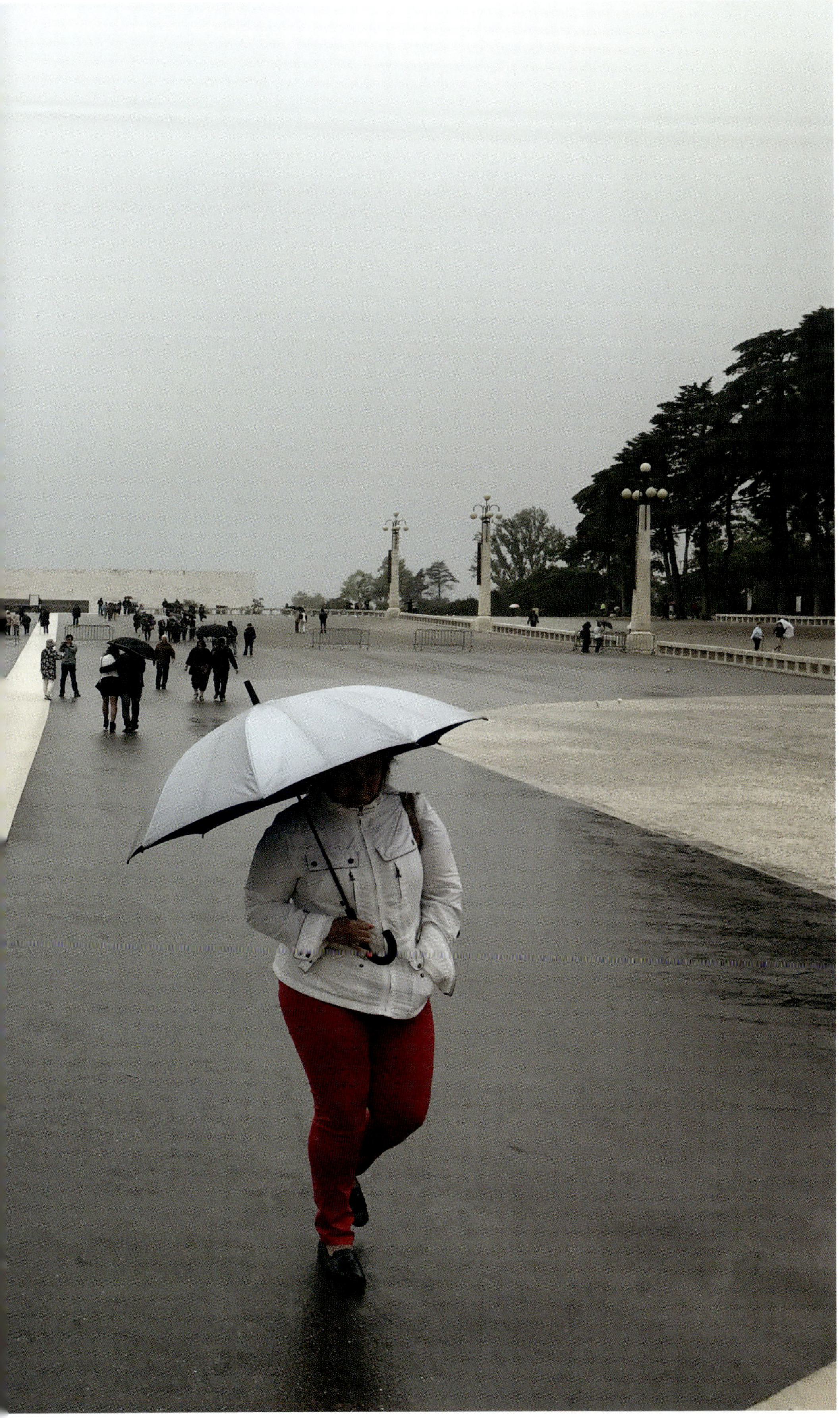

Fatima, Portugal, 2018

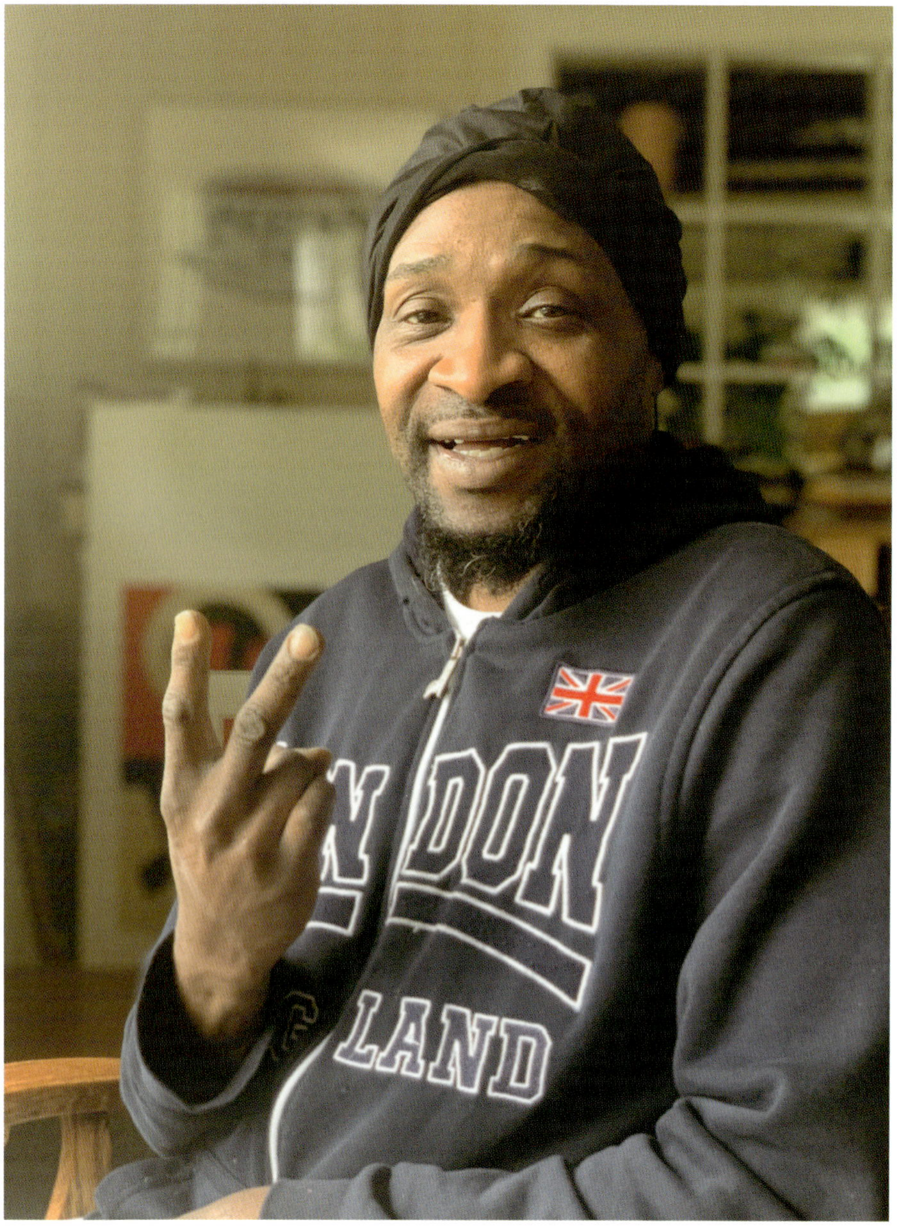

Jessie James Holman, 2022, (Valued Teammate and Sous Chef)

Acknowledgements

There have been numerous friends who have assisted in editing the words and pictures that make this book.

Leading the charge is Stephen Kobasa. Stephen was first to take note of my work. His editing, sequencing and exhibiting my prints was primary; he continues to support much that I do.

My partner, Corinne Forti, has been a major contributor in shaping this book. She is the source of the book's title; her skills with words and visual gifts are rare and much appreciated. I am blessed to have her support.

Robert Lisak has been a close friend and trusted critic for decades and has made invaluable suggestions regarding the text and sequence.

Eugenia Joyce Fayen has a laser sharp eye and pulls no punches in her criticism of pictures and words. I am indebted to her for an obsidian review.

Amos Chan is a dear friend and colleague. For many years, his generosity and extraordinary visual gifts have added much to the many projects we have shared.

Sven Martson, one of my oldest friends, sees what others often overlook. I am fortunate to have him as a colleague and a reviewer.

It is my good fortune to have Paige Onofreo as my gifted amanuensis. She transcribes faster than the speed of sound, and is generous with her prescient counsel.

Geoffrey Lawrence, my helper for years, brings an in-depth understanding of the nuance of word and image.

My exceptionally gifted opthomologist, Dr. Aron D. Rose, is to thank for keeping me in focus for so many years. His efforts have greatly extended my aging vision.

John T. Hill is a graphic designer, author and photographer. Hill was Norman Ives's student and teaching colleague at the Yale University School of Art where he taught both graphic design and photography. With Alvin Eisenman, Hill co-founded Yale's Department of Photography and was its first director of graduate studies.

Hill is currently focused on book and exhibition design, and writing. Two of his book designs were selected for the AIGA 50 Books of the Year Award.

During his nineteen year tenure as executor of the Walker Evans estate, Hill produced a number of books and exhibitions on this iconic artist. His comprehensive book *Walker Evans: Depth of Field*, was authored by Hill with essays by Heinz Liesbrock, director of the Josef Albers Museum Quadrat Bottrop.

Other books included *Walker Evans: At Work, Walker Evans: The Hungry Eye* and *Walker Evans: Lyric Documentary.*

Hill also designed, authored or co-authored many books of famous artists including *Calder by Matter, W. Eugene Smith Photographs, Edward Weston, Forms of Passion* and *May Day at Yale: Recollections 1970.*

In 2007 the AIGA hosted "Norman Ives: Constructions & Reconstructions," designed by Hill. This exhibit was Ives's first posthumous recognition as a fine artist and graphic designer.

R. Roger Remington, director of the Vignelli Center for Design Studies at The Rochester Institute of Technology, curated the exhibition Norman Ives: Constructions & Reconstructions. Remington and Hill mounted the first extensive showing of Ives's multi-faceted career.

In 2021 Hill curated two exhibitions of Ives's work following the publication of his in-depth chronicle of the spirit and genius of this master fine artist.

Hill recently authored *Herbert Matter: Artist Magician* that is being published by the Shanghai University Press.

BROWN'S
MULE

First edition published in 2022

Book design: John T. Hill
Separations by Steidl image department
Production and printing: Steidl, Göttingen

Steidl
Düstere Str. 4 / 37073 Göttingen, Germany
Phone +49 551 49 60 60
mail@steidl.de
steidl.de

ISBN 978-3-96999-176-3
Printed in Germany by Steidl